CHRISTCHURCH CHANGING

Christchurch Changing

An Illustrated History

GEOFFREY W. RICE

with assistance from
JEAN SHARFE

CANTERBURY UNIVERSITY PRESS

UNIVERSITY OF
CANTERBURY
CHRISTCHURCH · NEW ZEALAND

First published in 1999 by
CANTERBURY UNIVERSITY PRESS
University of Canterbury
Private Bag 4800
Christchurch
NEW ZEALAND

mail@cup.canterbury.ac.nz
www.cup.canterbury.ac.nz

Front cover: Corner of Lichfield, High and Colombo Streets
1906 postcard view from United Service Hotel
1999 view from ANZ Bank (Photograph by Duncan Shaw-Brown)
Half-title page: Staff of Dixon Brothers, Cash Butchers, Cashel Street, 1930s
(CM/CHAC 454)
Frontispiece: Chancery Lane, c. 1910 (CM 3616)
Back cover: View west along Worcester Boulevard from Cathedral tower, 1999.
Author photograph by Edwina Palmer

All unattributed photographs were taken by the author

Designed and typeset by Richard King
at Canterbury University Press
Printed by The Caxton Press, Christchurch

CONTENTS

'The poetry of history lies in the quasi-miraculous fact that once, on this earth, once, on this familiar spot of ground, walked other men and women, as actual as we are today, thinking their own thoughts, swayed by their own passions, but now all gone, one generation vanishing after another, gone as utterly as we ourselves shall shortly be gone, like ghosts at cock-crow.'

– G. M. Trevelyan, *Autobiography of an Historian*

22 April 1933: the Godley statue being moved back to its original position in Cathedral Square after fifteen years beside the Cathedral. Godley is not the only Christchurch statue to go walkabout: both Captain Cook and Queen Victoria were moved to new positions in Victoria Square in 1989.

PREFACE

The purpose of this book is to sketch the story of a major New Zealand city over the past hundred and fifty years, with enough photographs to show how much it has changed in that period of time. What was it like to live in this place in the 1850s, or the 1890s, or the 1940s? How did the city grow? What makes Christchurch distinctive among New Zealand's cities? What has changed, what has stayed put, what has been modified beyond recognition over a century and a half? Who were the key individuals who helped to shape outsiders' perceptions of Christchurch? These are just a few of the themes to be pursued.

The idea for this book originated in the History Department of the University of Canterbury. In 1992 Dr John Cookson (grandson of a previous mayor of Christchurch) conceived of a long-term research project that would produce a trio of books to mark the province's sesquicentennial in the year 2000. As we already had an excellent provincial history, and because much less work had been done on the city itself, the project was to be devoted to the metropolitan area of Christchurch, including the port of Lyttelton. With a research grant from the University of Canterbury, the 'Christchurch 2000 History Project' started in 1993.

The project's first priority was to establish what work had already been done, in both published and unpublished form, and what sources existed for further research on the city's history. Jean Sharfe was employed as a research assistant with the aim of constructing and maintaining an electronic database, listing and briefly describing every item, large or small, that she could find about Christchurch. As a result of her labours, the History Department now has an asset so far unique in New Zealand: a comprehensive descriptive list of over five thousand books, articles, theses, archive collections and manuscript sources for the history of a major New Zealand city.

Aware of the rich photographic archives of the Canterbury Museum (CM) and the Alexander Turnbull Library (ATL) in Wellington, we also wondered if there might be yet more treasures lurking in private collections or old family albums. With generous assistance from the Trustbank Canterbury Trust, the Lottery Grants Board and the Christchurch City Council, the project launched a public appeal in 1996 for historic photographs of Christchurch. Jean Sharfe played a key role in this Historic Photo Search, helped by Joan Woodward and a group of volunteers from the Canterbury Historical Association, in whose name the funding had been sought. Copy prints and all donated items were then deposited in the Pictorial Department of the Canterbury Museum, where they now form the Canterbury Historical Association Collection (CHAC).

Only a small selection of these images could be included in this book, however, as the great majority were domestic rather than public in nature. Canterbury Museum has provided most of the illustrations for the earlier chapters;

the *Christchurch Star* has been most generous in helping to augment the later chapters. Many of the photographs in this book have never been published before.

Right from the start, this book was meant to be an illustrated history rather than simply a picture book of Christchurch. The text had to be able to stand alone as a reliable narrative of major events and the larger developments that have made the city what it is today. In any case, there are several pictorial histories of Canterbury and Christchurch already available. By far the best of these is David Johnson's *Christchurch: A Pictorial History* (1992), also published by Canterbury University Press. This present book's official companion from the History Department's 'Christchurch 2000' project is *Southern Capital*, a volume of scholarly essays on various aspects of the city's history, edited by John Cookson and Graeme Dunstall.

There is still much to be discovered and explained about Christchurch's past, so these will certainly not be the last histories of the city to be published. There is such an abundance of visual and archival source material available that a book could be written about each of the following chapters. Although I have not seen every single item listed on Jean Sharfe's database, I am confident that I have read the most important ones, and several years' research for two other books have given me a close acquaintance with the files of *The Press* and *Lyttelton Times*. Even so, it is impossible to write a short history which will please all readers, and, in a city that loves controversy, whatever one says is likely to be contested. Here then, for what it is worth, is a personal view based on wide reading and forty-five years' residence in the 'Garden City'.

Acknowledgements

Many people have helped in the making of this book, and to all of them go my heartfelt thanks. The following deserve particular mention: Elizabeth Acland, Thérèse Angelo, Natalie Brittenden, Bill Browne, Daphne Cleveland, Bob Cotton, Dr John Gossett, Sir Hamish Hay, Elsie Locke, Jenny May, Patrick Holland and Jancis Meharry, Kerry McCarthy, Fiona Rice, James Murray, Bill Sutton, Lois Watson and Joan Woodward. Special thanks are due to Mike Fletcher for generously allowing us to use the photographic archives of the *Christchurch Star*. Dr John Cookson, Professor David McIntyre and Dr Edwina Palmer made helpful comments on earlier drafts, and Pauline Wedlake coped cheerfully with my numerous revisions. To my editor and designer, Richard King, I am especially grateful for making this such a good-looking book. Jean Sharfe's invaluable assistance with the illustrations and with the 'Christchurch 2000' project is recognised on the title page.

Geoffrey W. Rice
September 1999

CHAPTER ONE

The Town Imagined

Origins to 1852

The earliest human inhabitants of the area now covered by the city of Christchurch – Moa-hunters, or Archaic Phase Eastern Polynesians – probably arrived as early as AD 1000. At that time the coastal wetland was a thick forest of matai and totara, and parts of the Canterbury Plains may also have been forested. As well as killing off the moa (by about 1450), these earliest inhabitants also burned down forest. Any descendants of the Moa-hunters would have been killed or absorbed by migrating Classical Phase Maori from the North Island, most notably Ngati Mamoe and Ngai Tahu during the sixteenth and seventeenth centuries.

By the early nineteenth century the Ngai Turahuriri sub-tribe of Ngai Tahu controlled the coastal area between Te Waihora (Lake Ellesmere) and the Hurunui River. Their largest fortified pa, at Kaiapoi, may have held as many as a thousand people at its peak and was a major centre for trade in pounamu (greenstone) from the West Coast. Several smaller unfortified kainga, or seasonal settlements, were located within the present city boundaries, most notably at Putaringamotu (Riccarton) and Papanui, where isolated islands of tall forest had survived in a sea of tussock grassland and swamp.

'Rakawakaputa, Port Cooper Plains, 20 December 1848.' Watercolour by William Fox. A Maori village near the present site of Kaiapoi.

Hocken Library, Dunedin

Papanui

Wai-kakariki
(Horseshoe Lake)

**MAORI
PLACE NAMES OF
CHRISTCHURCH**

Otakaro (Avon River)

OTAUTAHI (Christchurch)

Putaringamotu (Riccarton Bush)

Rapanui (Shag Rock)

Tuawera (Cave Rock)

Matuku takotako (Sumner Beach)

Opawaho (Heathcote River)

*Te Onepoto
(Taylors Mistake)*

Te Tihi-o-Kahukura
(Castle Rock) ▲

Tauhinu-Korokio
▲ (Mount Pleasant)

Te Pohue (Sugar Loaf)

O-kete-upoko (Port Hills)

Awaroa (Godley Head)

*Ohinehou
(Cavendish Bay/Lyttelton)*

Puke-atua (Dyers Pass)

WHANGARAUPO (Lyttelton Harbour)

Te Rapaki (Rapaki Bay)

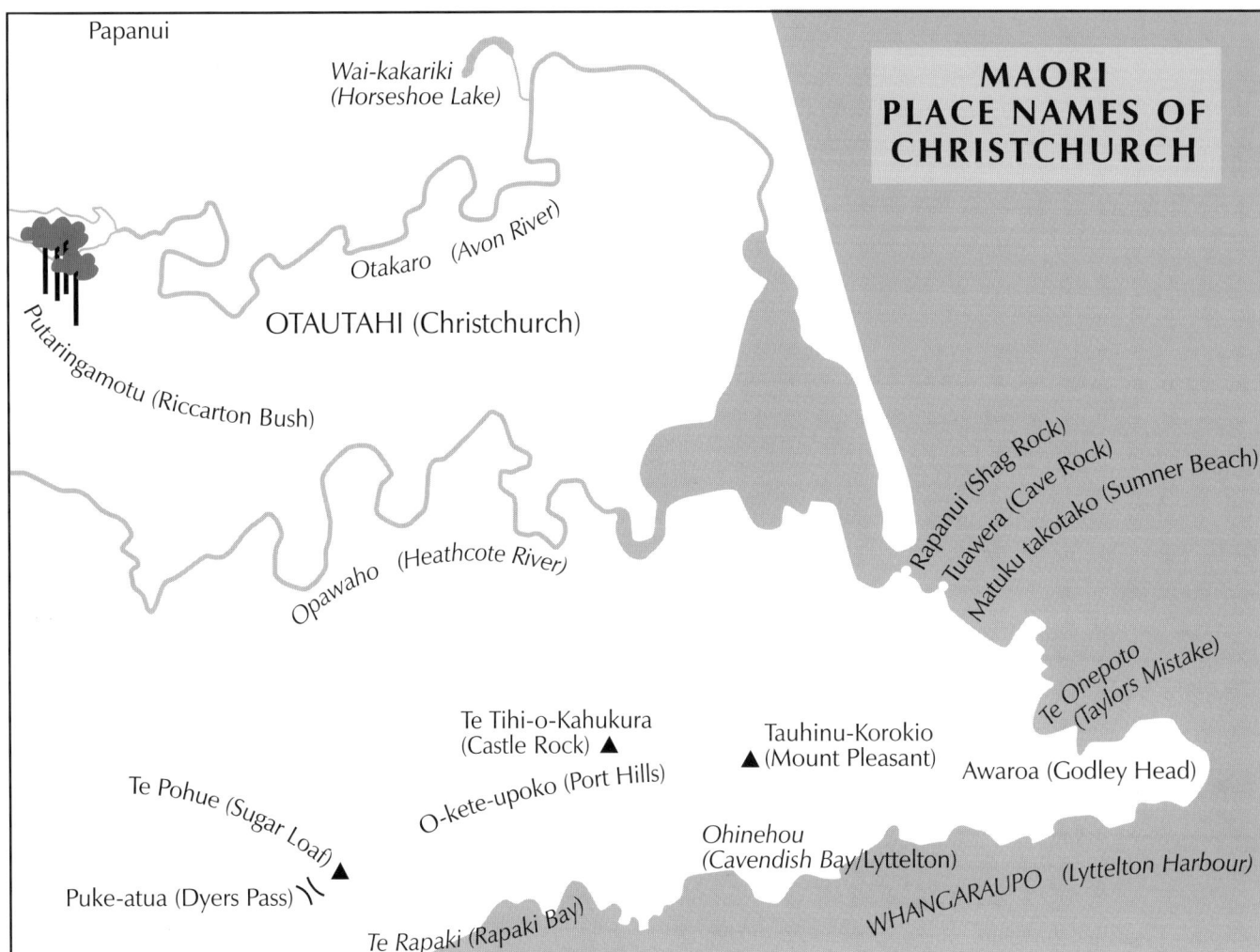

Possibly as many as five thousand Maori lived in central Canterbury by 1800, mostly at Kaiapoi and on Banks Peninsula, where the main settlements were at Akaroa, Puari (Port Levy), Purau and Rapaki. The main track between Kaiapoi and Rapaki passed through the heart of the present city, following sandy ridges through the swamps which then lay between the two main rivers, Otakaro (Avon) and Opawaho (Heathcote). Putaringamotu in particular was a valuable *mahinga kai*, or food-gathering place, with an abundance of birds, eels, fish and freshwater crayfish. The Maori name for Christchurch is Otautahi, 'the place of Tautahi', a Ngai Tahu chief who was buried near the present St Luke's Church vicarage around the 1750s.

The first Europeans known to set foot in Canterbury were from the sealing ship *Governor Bligh*, which spent a fortnight in one of the bays of Banks Peninsula about 1815. But the first to visit the site of what is now Christchurch stayed only long enough to bury one of their shipmates. In 1851 a wooden marker was found beside the remains of a skeleton in the New Brighton sandhills. It bore the initials H.L. and the date 1822, and was probably the grave of one of the flax-traders who visited Banks Peninsula from Australia in the 1820s. Another flax-trader, Captain William Wiseman, in 1827 gave the name Port Cooper to what is now Lyttelton Harbour. Whaling ships of various nationalities followed in the 1830s, and one of the earliest descriptions of the site of Christchurch is that of Captain W. B. (Barney) Rhodes, whose barque *Australian* visited Port Cooper in September 1836. He climbed to the nearest saddle of the Port Hills and saw a vast grassy plain with two small patches of forest (Riccarton and Papanui): 'All the land that I saw was swamp and mostly covered with water.'

Little wonder that the earliest European settlements in Canterbury were on Banks Peninsula rather than on the plains. Captain George Hempelman set up a permanent shore whaling station at Peraki in March 1837; his wife was the first white woman to live in Canterbury. Enthusiastic reports by French whalers aroused their government's interest in 'Nouvelle Zélande' as a possible site for colonisation, and a French warship, the *Héroine*, visited Akaroa Harbour in June 1838. The enterprising Captain Rhodes returned in November 1839 to land a herd of fifty cattle near Akaroa. There were about eighty Europeans settled on Banks Peninsula by 1840. By contrast, the Maori population of Canterbury had fallen dramatically to only about five hundred, as a result of a devastating civil war in the 1820s, destructive raids by Te Rauparaha in 1830 and 1832 (which destroyed Kaiapoi), and the deadly effects of new diseases, especially measles and influenza.

Christchurch was to be a British settlement, and what made New Zealand a British colony was the Treaty of Waitangi, first signed at the Bay of Islands on 6 February 1840. A few months later, Major Thomas Bunbury arrived at Akaroa on HMS *Herald* to gather signatures to the Treaty from Ngai Tahu. Then, in August 1840, Captain Owen Stanley came on HMS *Britomart* to raise the Union Jack at Akaroa, barely a week before sixty-three French colonists arrived on the *Comte de Paris*. European settlement continued to be concentrated on the peninsula rather than the plains.

The first European settlers within the present boundaries of Christchurch were two small groups of farmers who arrived from Sydney in April 1840, led by James Herriot, whose backers had bought over 7,000 acres from one George Weller, believing that he had bought the land from Ngai Tahu. Their first crop was successful, but they were so discouraged by a plague of rats that they gave up after a single season.

The second attempt at European settlement on the plains was much more successful. William and John Deans were well-educated Scottish farmers who decided to settle in Canterbury in 1843 after being disappointed with the land allotted to them by the New Zealand Company in Wellington and Nelson. William arrived at Port Cooper in February, with the Gebbie and Manson families, who were to be their farm workers. From Lyttelton they came round to the Estuary and took a whaleboat up the River Avon to a point near the present Barbadoes Street bridge, where they unloaded some bricks they had brought to build a chimney. (For many years this place was known as 'The Bricks', where early settlers off-loaded their heavy luggage.) The river then became so shallow and overgrown that the party had to change to a canoe. Finally they reached a pool near the present site of Christchurch Girls' High School, where they unloaded the rest of their timber and supplies. These were carried through fern and raupo to the patch of forest known as Puta-ringamotu, where they discovered the remains of the barley stacks abandoned by Herriot. Here the Deans brothers built the first European house on the plains, in three compartments for the three families in their party. (It was held together with wooden pegs, as the nails had been left behind in Wellington.) They named their farm Riccarton,

John Deans I (1820–54) and his brother William were pioneers of the Canterbury Plains at Putaringamotu, which they renamed Riccarton.
CM 16206

Jane Deans (1823–1911), widowed in 1854, devoted the rest of her life to her son John Deans II and the Riccarton estate. She was a staunch member of Christchurch's Presbyterian community, helping to establish St Andrew's Church in 1857. She ensured the preservation of Riccarton Bush.
CM 16205

Deans brothers' farm at Riccarton (Putaringamotu), November 1850. Pencil sketch by H. J. Cridland, facsimile by E. M. Hocken.

CM 3886 A

Edward Gibbon Wakefield (1796–1862), charming manipulator, convicted abductor, theorist of systematic colonisation, colonial promoter and politician. Canterbury, of all the New Zealand settlements, came closest to his ideal of transplanting 'a slice of England' to a new land.

CM 1538

after their home parish near Kilmarnock, in Ayrshire, and the river the Avon, after a stream on their grandfather's farm.

The success of the Deans brothers' farm at Riccarton greatly influenced the siting of the principal town of the Canterbury settlement. The farm was still not fully established when Frederick Tuckett visited in April 1844, in search of a suitable site for a Scottish settlement in New Zealand; dismayed by the swamps, he opted for Otago instead. But the Deans brothers' laden fruit trees and enormous carrots reassured later surveyors that the settlers would not starve. On 7 January 1844 the first European child born within the present area of Christchurch (Jeannie Manson) made her appearance at Riccarton, but in the following year her parents left with the Gebbies to establish their own farm at the head of Lyttelton Harbour. Also settled on the harbour were the Greenwood brothers at Purau, who were the victims of Canterbury's first armed robbery in 1846. Little wonder that they moved on, after selling Purau to the Rhodes brothers.

In November 1847, far away in England, an idealistic young Anglo-Irish lawyer, John Robert Godley, met the famous theorist of colonisation Edward Gibbon Wakefield to plan another settlement in New Zealand. The result was the formation of the Canterbury Association early in 1848, supported by an illustrious body of peers, members of Parliament and clergy of the Church of England, including the Archbishop of Canterbury. Godley and the Association's chairman, Lord Lyttelton, were the key members of a small committee which organised the new colony. Its capital city was to be named Christ Church, after Godley's Oxford College.

Canterbury was the most successful of Wakefield's colonisation schemes, and the one that came closest to his ideal of transplanting a cross-section of English society to the other side of the world. Wakefield's concept of colonisation was strongly urban. He deplored the disorder and uncivilised behaviour of frontier colonies, and insisted that his settlements were to have a well-established town, with all the amenities of civilised society, as the hub of a farming community. He and Godley envisaged a compact agricultural settlement of carefully selected Anglican families, with a cathedral and college at the heart of its future capital city. Land would be sold at a 'sufficient price' to provide endowments for public works and a lavish provision of schools, churches and clergy. But first the land had to be bought from its Maori owners.

Governor Grey sent Commissioner Henry Kemp to the South Island in 1848 to purchase land for settlement. Despite much disagreement and misunderstanding, sixteen Ngai Tahu chiefs agreed to sign 'Kemp's Deed' at Akaroa in 12 June, selling the greater part of their land for £2,000 (to be paid in instalments) but reserving their settlements and food-gathering places and claiming larger reserves of land once the surveying was done. Unfortunately, the deed did not correspond to Charles Kettle's attached sketch map, and this caused yet more confusion and friction. Tikao (John Love) had suggested £5 million as a more realistic value for Ngai Tahu's lands, but Kemp had only been authorised to offer £2,000. Later in 1848 Walter Mantell came to conduct the survey, but he largely ignored Ngai Tuahuriri requests for large blocks of land as reserves; instead he marked out a mere 1,068 hectares at Tuahiwi before travelling south to Otago. Mantell deliberately reduced the reserves, allowing less than four acres per head instead of the promised ten. He even denied Ngai Tahu some of their cultivated land and most of their mahinga kai. The promised reserves never materialised, and Ngai Tahu rightly concluded that they had been cheated by the Crown. Although they were soon to be marginalised by the arrival of thousands of British settlers, they never gave up their claim for compensation.

Captain Joseph Thomas, a pioneer of Wellington in 1840 and an experienced surveyor who had travelled the entire length of New Zealand, was sent to choose a site for the Canterbury Association's settlement. He had £20,000 to complete a survey and make preparations for the arrival of the first migrants. Thomas arrived at Lyttelton Harbour in December 1848 with William Fox and surveyors Thomas Cass and Charles Torlesse. They were later joined by Edward

Captain Joseph Thomas (1803–1880?), army officer, engineer, and surveyor of Wanganui, Porirua, Hawke's Bay, Otago and Canterbury settlements. Bluff, quick-tempered and autocratic, he quarrelled with Godley over the cost of the road works from Lyttelton to Sumner, and was dismissed in January 1851. He later worked for a mining company in Australia, but his last years are shrouded in mystery.

Alexander Turnbull Library, Wellington

George William Lyttelton (right), 4th Baron Lyttelton (1817–76), chairman of the Canterbury Association and Under-Secretary for the Colonies (1846). Seen here in Dr Barker's garden with Henry Selfe Selfe, February 1868.

CM ACB 4/1

Jollie. Thomas had previously selected the head of Port Cooper as the obvious site for a town, but when he realised how much reclamation would be needed to provide the 4,000 hectares required by the Association, he switched to a second site, marked as 'Stratford' on his original sketch map. This was to become Christchurch, and though the Pilgrims of 1850 grumbled about its swampiness, the site was an obvious compromise between the limits of boat navigation on the Avon, the nearest elevated dry land to the coast, and the nearest sources of timber at Riccarton and Papanui.

Thomas had hoped to locate the port for the new colony at Rapaki, but its Maori inhabitants were reluctant to part with their recently allotted reserve, so he chose a bay nearer the sea (Erskine, or Cavendish Bay) and began to build a jetty and a custom house. So was founded the port of Lyttelton. About eighty labourers and carpenters were brought down from Wellington, and Thomas hired another hundred (at least half were Maori) from Banks Peninsula. During 1849 and 1850 these men built houses and barracks for the settlers, and started to form a road to Sumner via Evans Pass, until funds ran out and work stopped. An alternative track, desperately steep in places, went up the hill behind the town and over the saddle to Heathcote Valley. This 'Bridle Path' was to be the Pilgrims' main route to their promised land.

The appointed leader of the Canterbury settlement, John Robert Godley, arrived at Lyttelton on the *Lady Nugent* on 12 April 1850. At first he was delighted by what he saw: roads being formed, two dozen houses finished, the Immigration Barracks almost ready. But once ashore he quarrelled with Captain Thomas

Detail of Captain Thomas's 1849 map, showing Lyttelton as Port Victoria, Christchurch at the head of the harbour and Stratford as the principal city of the Canterbury settlement, beside the Deans' farm at Riccarton.

CM 11024

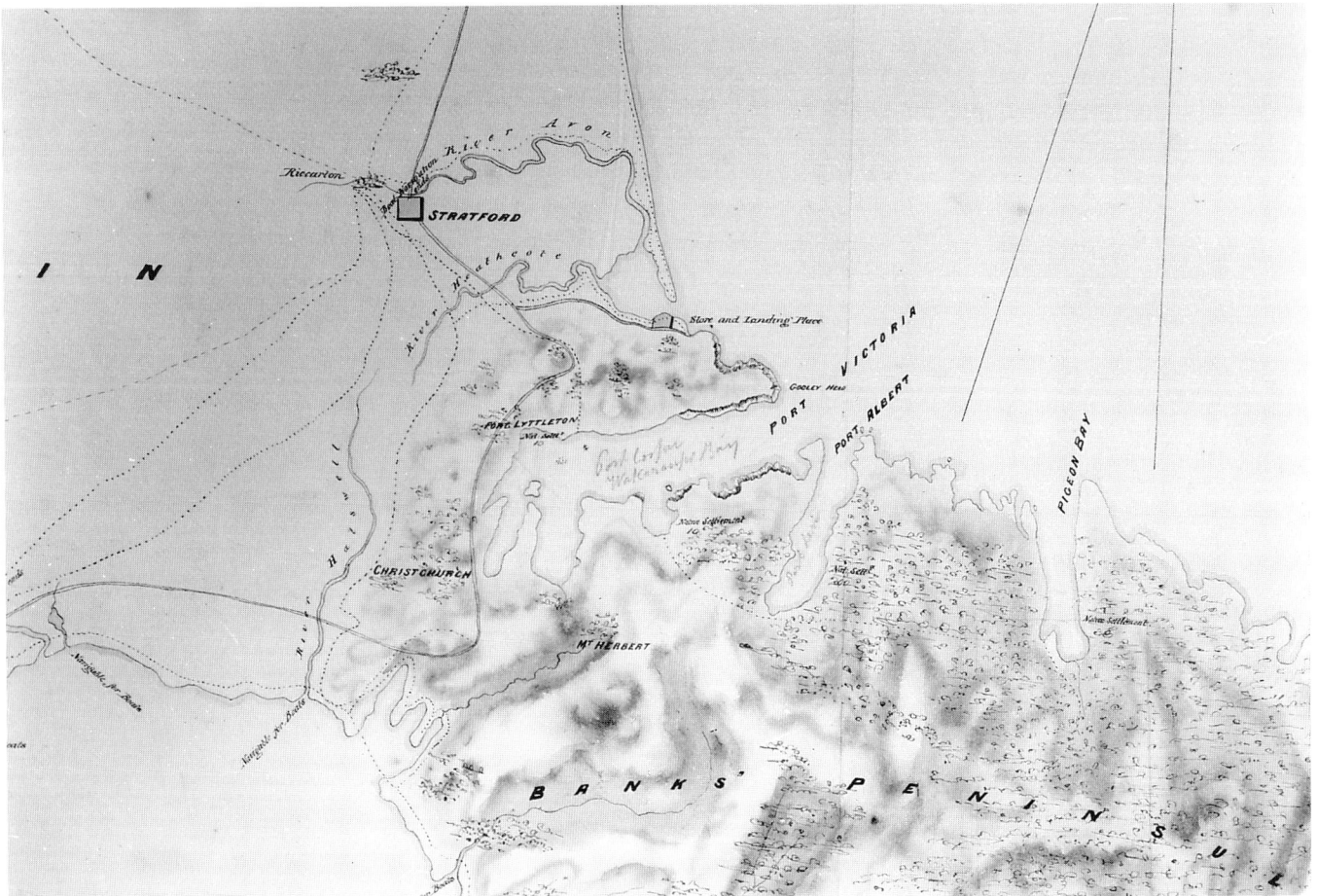

over the cost of it all, and confirmed the stoppage of work on the Sumner Road. After only two days, Godley departed for Wellington, where he also quarrelled with Governor Grey. The two men took an instant dislike to each other, and disagreed sharply over land policy. Godley had been dismayed to find 'Scotch Presbyterians' already settled on the best land adjacent to his proposed Anglican capital, and had refused to grant the Deans brothers the pastoral land they needed on the plains.

Although Godley is generally regarded as 'the Founder of Canterbury', Christchurch owes a great deal to Captain Thomas. He surveyed the site and laid out the streets. His assistant, Jollie, left a delightful description of this process: 'Thomas with his gold spectacles on and a Peerage in his hand read out a name he fancied and if he thought it sounded well and I also thought so, it was written on the map.' Jollie had proposed several crescents, which Thomas had rejected as 'gingerbread', so the city was laid out as a simple grid, broken only by the diagonals formed by High Street and Victoria Street, linking the town respectively to Ferry Road and Papanui Bush. Ironically, what was to become the most English of colonial cities was laid out like any new town of North America. The best-known names of English dioceses had already been used on the map of Lyttelton, leaving a mixture of lesser English, Irish, Welsh and colonial dioceses for Christchurch. One striking feature of the plan, for which succeeding generations would be eternally grateful, was the provision of a large open space, named Hagley Park, after one of Lord Lyttelton's estates.

The Canterbury Association had bought the land for its settlement from the New Zealand Company and, in accordance with Wakefield's theory of the 'sufficient price', offered intending colonists rural sections in lots of not less than 50 acres (20 hectares) at £3 per acre. Purchasers had to be members of the Church of England and 'of good character'. The capital city of 1,000 acres was to be divided into quarter-acre sections, which would be drawn in a ballot by their purchasers on arrival in the new land. Purchasers would also have rights of pasturage over unoccupied land. The Association hoped to sell 100,000 acres to cover its expenses and establish a colony of fifteen thousand people, with a bishop, twenty-one clergy and twenty schoolmasters.

By 1 July 1850 only about 9,000 acres had been sold, and Godley's friends had to raise substantial sums of money to save the project. However, the Association succeeded in attracting colonists with a good range of useful occupations. Twelve shiploads were planned, and the first four of these were ready to sail from Gravesend in September 1850. A farewell banquet impressed one newspaper reporter, who later wrote: 'A slice of England, cut from top to bottom, was despatched to the Antipodes . . .'

'The First Four Ships' have become part of Canterbury's foundation myth. To be descended from one of these first 'Pilgrims' still carries a certain social cachet in some Christchurch circles, but there were many more such ships and, as we have seen, their passengers were far from being the first Europeans to settle in Canterbury. One thing that may have helped create the myth of the First Four Ships is the remarkable fact that they all arrived at Lyttelton so close together after three months of solitary voyaging around the globe. The *Charlotte Jane* arrived on the morning of 16 December 1850, and the *Randolph* at mid-afternoon that same day; the *Sir George Seymour* arrived next day, and the *Cressy*

John Robert Godley (1814–1861), founder of the Canterbury settlement; lawyer, writer, coloniser, administrator and public servant. Founder (with Wakefield) of the Canterbury Association, he spent 1850–52 as the effective governor of the little settlement, 'like a whale in a duck-pond'. He was later Assistant Under-Secretary at the War Office in London.
CM 713

15

ten days later. Godley was there to meet them, with Sir George and Lady Grey.

The first Pilgrim ashore was James Edward FitzGerald. Dr Alfred Barker (future photographer of the new settlement) was determined to be the 'first-footer' and had commandeered the prow of the rowing boat, but the ebullient FitzGerald simply leapfrogged over him. Behind FitzGerald, impatient to set their feet on dry land, were altogether 773 colonists. More than two hundred of these were single men and women: the agricultural labourers, shepherds and domestic serv-

Canterbury Association emigration poster, 1850.

CM

Lyttelton, 10 January 1851. Sketch by William Fox, showing Godley's house (centre, with gables and verandah) and the Immigration Barracks.
CM

ants of Wakefield's plan. There were also carpenters, blacksmiths, barbers, plumbers, gardeners, bricklayers, printers, stonemasons and one butcher. Visiting Australian pastoralists, looking for cheap land, were amused by the number of pianos brought with them by the Canterbury Pilgrims.

After months at sea, the Pilgrims yearned for fresh meat and vegetables. The Deans brothers could supply both, but from a distance. For the summer months of 1850–51, Lyttelton was mainly provisioned by the Rhodes brothers from Purau. Every week they rowed a whaleboat across the harbour, laden with fresh mutton and vegetables. Local Maori soon found that the settlers would pay £6 a ton for potatoes, and they did a roaring trade.

The Pilgrims' first impressions of Lyttelton were doubtless coloured by their relief at having arrived safely; many were surprised to see so many buildings and a large 'Yankee' jetty. The ships stayed in port for several weeks while luggage was unloaded. Apart from the Immigration Barracks, many Pilgrims lived in tents or V-huts. Fortunately the fine summer weather held until everyone was ashore. Some had brought prefabricated frames for their houses as cargo on the ships. These could not be dragged over the steep Bridle Path and, like all heavy luggage, had to be sailed round to the Estuary, to be taken up the Avon to Christchurch.

Although Thomas and Jollie had marked out the ground plan of the future city, most of the streets were no more than ploughed furrows through the tussock and toetoe when the first Pilgrims arrived. The first 'selection days' were held in February 1851 at the Land Office (on the banks of the Avon, where S. Hurst Seager's 1887 Municipal Chambers building now stands). Each purchase of 20 hectares of rural land gave the purchaser a free grant of a town section. Not surprisingly, most of the first town sections chosen were in Lyttelton

17

'V-huts at Milford, Papanui Road, 1864.' Photograph by Dr Barker, probably near the present site of St George's Hospital.
CM

rather than in Christchurch, as it was already a real and prosperous town, unlike the imagined town over the hill.

Not all of the colonists liked the name 'Christ Church', which sounded 'too churchy': most preferred the 'good English name' Lyttelton, and at first the land sales documents used the name Lyttelton for both the port and the town on the plains. Confusion persisted until 10 June 1851, when the Colonists' Council resolved to call the town on the plains 'Christchurch', as fixed by Captain Thomas and his surveyors.

What was it like to be one of the first residents of Christchurch in 1851? Conscious that they were making history, many of the Pilgrims wrote about their experiences in letters to family or friends back in England, and some of their accounts are understandably selective or romanticised. (Everyone remembered the spectacular sunsets in the clear air of that first year in Canterbury.) A more realistic description, based on his diary, was published in 1893 by John Buchanan, a Scot who was sixteen years old when he arrived in February 1851. His first nights in the immigration barracks in Lyttelton were not very pleasant: 'the fleas were numerous and lively'. His shipboard friends confided their feelings of loneliness in the vast open spaces of the new land. One was so homesick that he soon returned to England. The nights were very dark, with unfamiliar bird calls. Until wooden houses could be built, many of the Pilgrims lived in primitive shelters made from thatched raupo or toetoe, daubed with mud. There was no shortage of mud, or of rain in the winter of 1851. These shelters soon became infested with rats. On rainy days, when no work could be done, rat hunts were a favourite pastime, as was taking pot shots with a rifle at ducks on the Avon. Laundry was a terrible chore for the women. Boots and trousers could be quickly reduced to ribbons by the abrasive toetoe. Horses were scarce in the new settlement, so everyone had to walk, often carrying bags or boxes, or dragging the timber for houses and fences.

The Pilgrims had brought with them seeds of all kinds and, like the Deans brothers, found the soil exceptionally fertile, at least for the first crop. Rather than scatter precious seed for the birds to eat, the new settlers planted wheat and barley crops by 'dibbling', one grain per hole. Many counted their tree seedlings as they appeared – hawthorn, oak, plane, laburnum – only to find them trampled next morning by wandering cattle. Keeping warm and dry were not easy tasks in the winter of 1851. In the absence of bridges, crossing the Avon without a boat was always hazardous. But nobody stayed wet for long. The 'dazzling sunlight' soon dried things out, and gradually a town began to take shape where wilderness had previously prevailed.

Inevitably, 1851 was a year of firsts in the Canterbury settlement. On 6 January the province's first school opened in Lyttelton, under the Reverend Henry Jacobs, and the Collegiate Grammar School (later Christ's College) followed in April, both in the Immigration Barracks. On 11 January the first copy of the *Lyttelton Times* was printed, having been edited and largely written by J. E. Fitz-Gerald. A week later the Union Bank of Australasia opened at Lyttelton. In February Christchurch's first footbridge was built across the Avon at Worcester Street, beside the Land Office, where the first sale of town sections was held on 16 April. George Gould opened his general store on Colombo Street, facing Market Square, on 3 May, and later that month the Ferrymead ferry service commenced operations. A cricket club was formed on 21 June, and a month later the first church service was held in a small wooden chapel later consecrated as St Michael and All Angels'. In September the first drowning in the Avon was recorded (the victim was drunk), and in November the first hotel – the White Hart in High Street – opened, to replace the canvas grog-shops.

Even so, to most of its residents Christchurch was still a 'howling wilderness', especially when the hot nor'westers blew. Dr Barker recalled meeting a

'The Canterbury Plains, 1851.' Plate 4 from *A Spring in the Canterbury Settlement* by C. W. Adams (London, 1853). Viewed from St Andrews Hill. Drawing by William Howard Holmes, engraved by H. Adlard. The original key is as follows: '1. Southern Alps, distant 100 miles but from the clearness of the atmosphere distinctly visible. 2. Harewood Forest and Oxford. Near this spot coal has been found. 3. Riccarton Bush. 4. Christchurch. 5. Papenui Bush [sic]. 6. 7. Sand Hills, amongst which wild Pigs are found. 8. Heathcote River. 9. Bridle Path. 10. New Road to Christchurch [Ferry Road]. 11. Christchurch Quay [Radley Wharf]. 12. Greenlands – S. Townsend, Esq. 13. Swamps.'
CM 11023

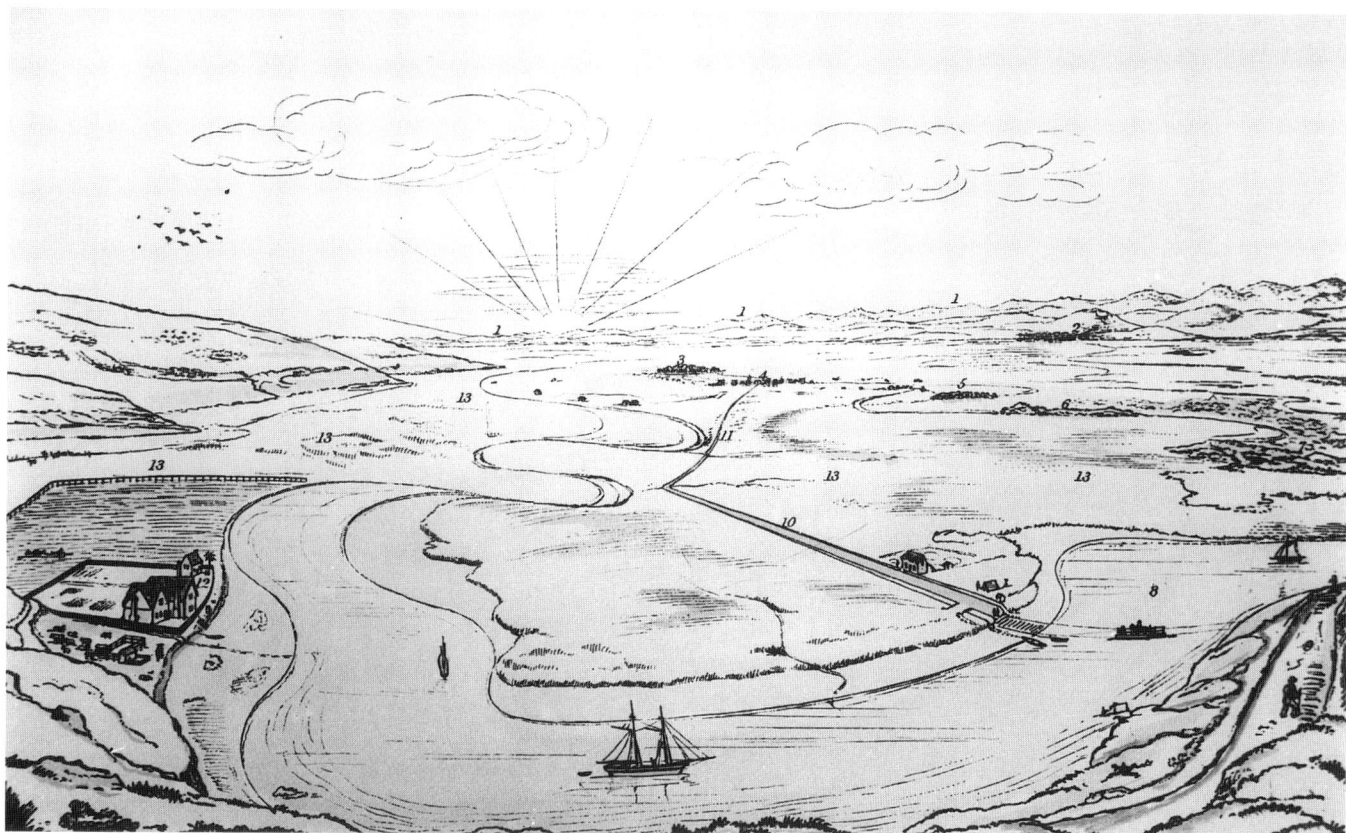

Above: 'Studdingsail Hall, Christchurch, New Zealand,' 23 January 1851. Dr Alfred Barker's first dwelling. Note the packing cases and outdoor cooking arrangements.

CM 5396

Right: 'Interior of Studdingsail Hall,' 27 February 1851. Sketch by Dr Barker. His wife appears distinctly unimpressed by her makeshift surroundings, despite the clock and elegant table.

CM

man near his house, struggling through the tall flax and scrub of Cathedral Square, who demanded to be shown the way to Christchurch!

By the time Canterbury's first anniversary was celebrated, on 16 December 1851, with athletics and a cricket match, the First Four Ships had been followed by eight chartered Canterbury Association ships and seven private ventures, bringing the population of the settlement to three thousand. Many of these new arrivals did not stay long in Lyttelton or Christchurch, however, but dispersed over the plains. Godley had soon realised that the plains were ideal for pastoral farming, and that the original plan for a close-knit agricultural settlement was unworkable. He lobbied successfully to ease the restrictions placed on pastoral leases by the Canterbury Association, and in August 1851 an Act was passed enabling the Association to make its own regulations. Early in 1852 more favourable leases were issued, with a sliding scale for rent which rose as the flocks increased. Godley's alteration saved the Canterbury settlement from economic suicide and attracted experienced pastoralists from Australia who brought both sheep and capital to transform the settlement's economic prospects and shape the early growth of Christchurch. The runholders gave Canterbury its first and major export: wool. Christchurch first grew as the market town for a pastoral economy.

The Victorian gold rush in Australia suddenly drained the Canterbury settlement of its young single men early in 1852. The resulting labour shortage had a serious effect on public works, slowing development for the next three years. On 30 June 1852 the New Zealand Constitution Act was passed by the Westminster Parliament, dividing New Zealand into six provinces, each with its own administration. The Canterbury Association ceased to exist as from 30 September. Godley was invited to become the province's first superintendent, but he declined, having decided to return to England. His departure in December 1852 marked the end of Christchurch's pioneering phase. In two years the Pilgrims and their fellow migrants had established a town (admittedly somewhat resembling a shanty town) and had founded a province soon to become one of the wealthiest in colonial New Zealand.

Godley's achievement was remarkable, considering all the problems he faced, while the Canterbury Association's legacy to the city of Christchurch was fundamental. It is thanks to them that the city has its present physical plan, of a grid pattern of streets and the great open space of Hagley Park. But it is also thanks to the Canterbury Association that Christchurch was to be a cathedral city, with many churches and a grammar school. Their most influential legacy was a set of values and ideals that gave Christchurch a distinctive character and opinion of itself, which endured for a full century after the pioneering phase.

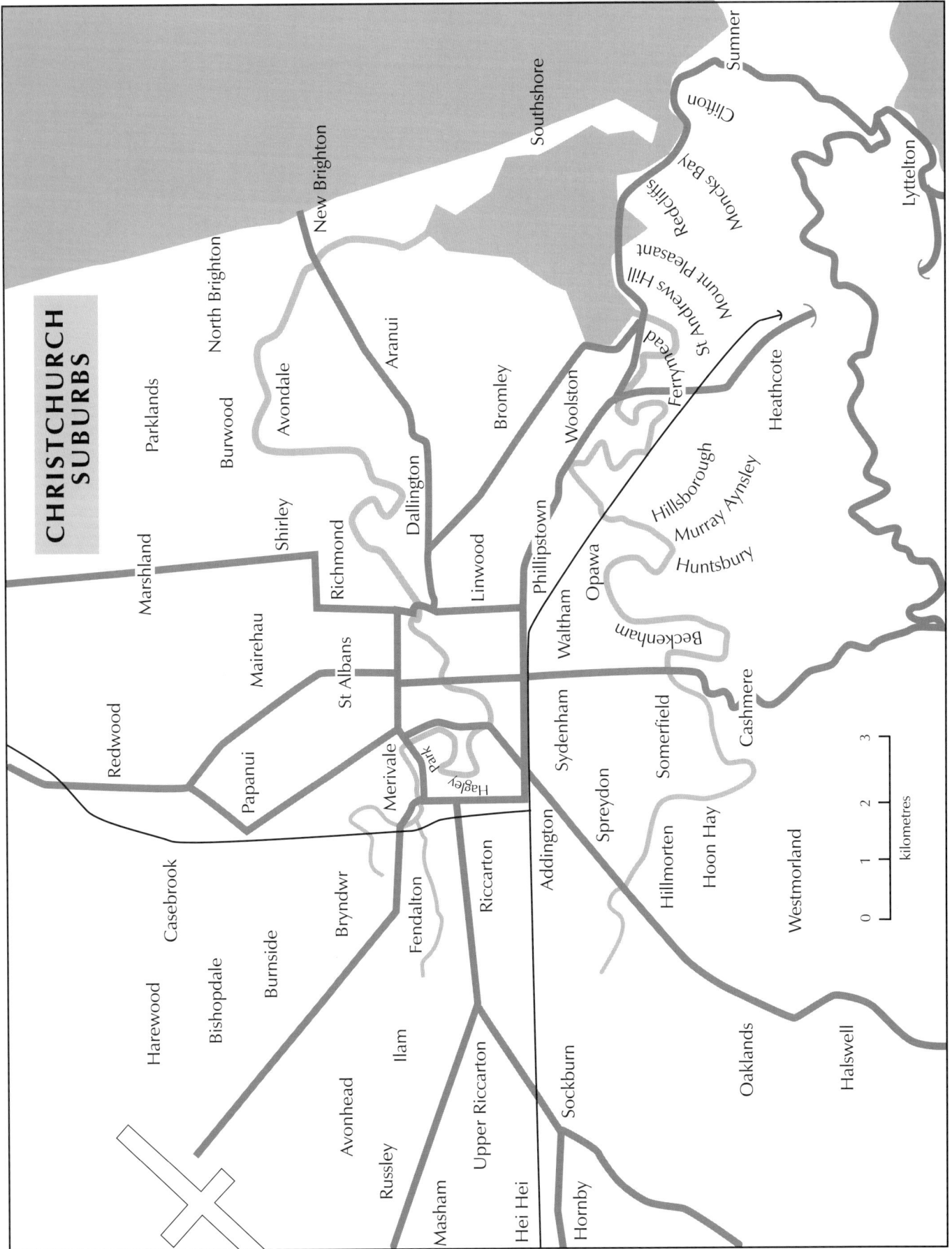

CHRISTCHURCH SUBURBS

Sumner
Clifton
Lyttelton
Southshore
New Brighton
Redcliffs
Moncks Bay
North Brighton
Mount Pleasant
St Andrews Hill
Parklands
Aranui
Ferrymead
Heathcote
Burwood
Avondale
Bromley
Woolston
Marshland
Shirley
Richmond
Dallington
Hillsborough
Murray Aynsley
Linwood
Phillipstown
Huntsbury
St Albans
Mairehau
Opawa
Waltham
Beckenham
Redwood
Papanui
Merivale
Hagley Park
Sydenham
Somerfield
Cashmere
Casebrook
Bryndwr
Fendalton
Riccarton
Addington
Spreydon
Hillmorten
Hoon Hay
Westmorland
Harewood
Bishopdale
Burnside
Ilam
Upper Riccarton
Sockburn
Oaklands
Halswell
Avonhead
Russley
Masham
Hei Hei
Hornby

0 1 2 3
kilometres

CHAPTER TWO

Frontier Town

1853 – 1876

Godley's departure left many of the Canterbury Pilgrims in low spirits. They had no bishop, and now they had no leader. It was little wonder that new arrivals felt disheartened, standing among the tussock on the site of the future cathedral. There were far more open spaces than buildings; plenty of street names but no proper streets; plenty of clergy but not enough churches. In short, everything had been started but nothing finished. Lyttelton was still the largest town, with about eight hundred inhabitants in 1852, but the demographic balance then changed rapidly. By 1854 Christchurch had a population of 924 (in 183 houses) and Lyttelton only 548 (in 109 houses). Christchurch was still confined within the boundaries of Barbadoes, St Asaph, Salisbury and Antigua Streets, but Godley's 'town reserves' began to be sold in 1855, and had all been snapped up by 1858. Christchurch's further growth depended on the province's economic prospects.

Edward Jollie's 1850 plan of central Christchurch, showing Godley's Town Reserves, Hagley Park and the Government Domain (now the Botanic Gardens).

CM 4296

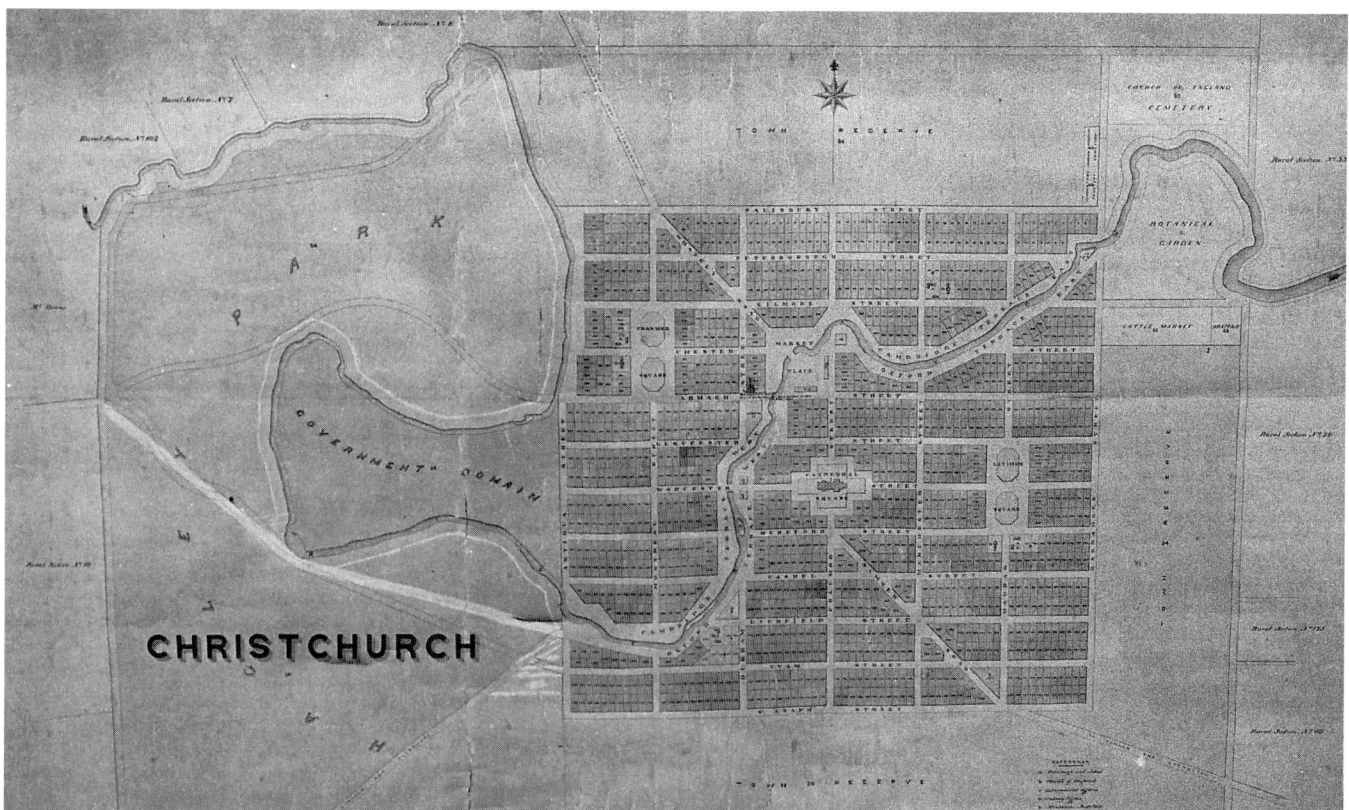

These were not very bright in 1853. The last of the Canterbury Association's immigrants arrived that year, and some of the single men took one look and sailed off to the Victorian goldfields. The province's economy stagnated in the early 1850s. Lack of labour delayed building, and lack of roads hampered exports. There was even some serious talk of importing Chinese labourers on contract, but this did not win general approval. At least by 1854 the settlement was feeding itself, from a green belt of surrounding small farms, and producing a modest surplus. Now that they were properly settled, the Pilgrims could think about such things as government and politics.

New Zealand had a split-level system of government during the provincial period (1853–76). The Governor and General Assembly comprised the central government, responsible to the Colonial Office in London for legislation, defence, native affairs, harbours, coinage and suchlike, while everything else was left to six provincial governments, each with an elected superintendent and council. It was not meant to be a federal system, but difficult communications between widely scattered settlements made it quasi-federal in practice. Governor Grey saw fit to introduce the provincial level first, which gave Canterbury the chance to set up a miniature parliament rather than just a glorified municipality. Provincial governments were keen to control as much of their own business as they could, especially in the key area of land policy.

Only four superintendents held office in Canterbury during the provincial period – FitzGerald, Moorhouse, Bealey and Rolleston – and their names were later given to the four wide avenues or 'belts' that enclosed the original town. The Provincial Council initially had twelve members, but later grew to thirty-nine, and a total of 166 men served at various times on the council. Most of Christchurch's nascent elite took their turn at provincial politics, and took them-

Part of Dr Barker's 1860 panorama of Christchurch, taken from the tower of the Provincial Council Buildings. The view is south-east across Oxford Terrace and Gloucester Street. The foreground is now occupied by the Canterbury Public Library. In the middle distance, part of Cathedral Square has been fenced and planted to form a public garden.

Dr A. C. Barker photograph, CM

Detail from Dr Barker's 1860 panorama. View towards the west, with Christ's College in the middle distance and Deans Bush on the horizon to the right.

CM 286

selves very seriously as they did so. Yet this was no gathering of greybeards. Most were young men or in the prime of their thirties and forties. Many of them lived in Christchurch, but the executive tended to be dominated by runholders and farmers. Their priorities were immigration, roads, bridges and (later) railways, to develop the province as a whole, which often gave grounds for complaint that the Provincial Council did too little for the growing city.

Christchurch was controlled by the Canterbury Provincial Council until a town board was set up in 1862 (which became the Christchurch City Council six years later), so there was intense public interest in the early elections for the superintendent and council. James Edward FitzGerald was Canterbury's first superintendent (1853–57). More a visionary than a practical administrator, he

On the left of this Dr Barker photograph, entitled 'The Argument', is James Edward FitzGerald (1818–96). Emigration agent, journalist and founding editor of the *Lyttelton Times*, he was Canterbury's first superintendent (1853–57). He also founded *The Press* in 1861, but moved to Wellington in 1867 as Comptroller of Public Accounts. He was a brilliant speaker and a talented artist. His statue is at the hospital end of Rolleston Avenue. At right is William Rolleston (1831–1903), Canterbury's fourth superintendent (1868–76), who arrived at Lyttelton in 1858 and worked as a cadet at Lake Coleridge before buying his own sheep station at Rakaia Forks. His statue stands in front of the Canterbury Museum on Rolleston Avenue.

CM 416f

25

nevertheless had abundant energy and an Irishman's gift for oratory. In his speech opening the first session of the Provincial Council on 27 September 1853 (in an empty printing office in the middle of a potato patch), FitzGerald reminded the Canterbury Pilgrims of the high ideals behind their settlement and the principles that should guide its government. Even though the council took all of the first session to settle the machinery of government, this was no small achievement, for it then worked well with little alteration until 1876.

The big issue facing the new Provincial Council was land policy, especially control of the so-called 'waste lands' outside the original Canterbury Association block. Godley had feared that if they were sold cheaply this would only encourage sheepfarming and disperse settlement, thus undermining Wakefield's ideal of a compact agricultural colony. FitzGerald saw early on that sheep farming was the only way to make money quickly in Canterbury, and he was not the only one. Experienced Australian pastoralists, nicknamed 'Shagroons' by the Pilgrims, were eyeing the Canterbury back country as ideal for sheep. At the time much was said about the conflict between the Pilgrims and the Shagroons, though this was more literary than actual. There was plenty of land for all, but Governor Grey's 1853 waste-land regulations set a price that Canterbury leaders thought far too low, and they won a court injunction to get them suspended. Grey ignored the ruling and was never again trusted by Cantabrians. However, the rapid sale of back-country runs gave the Provincial Council its first steady revenue, and the sheep were soon to save the province's economy.

Christchurch was an important social centre for the pastoral runholders, as well as a source of supplies and a place to find banks and lawyers. In the same month that Joseph Palmer opened the Union Bank, March 1856, a group of runholders formed the Christchurch Club, to provide congenial accommodation along the lines of an English gentlemen's club. Many of the early runholders were university graduates, and some came from titled English families. This led outsiders to label Canterbury 'that aristocratic province', and one historian to write of 'a southern gentry'. But the runholders had to be practical and work hard to succeed, and most of them did. Their sheep certainly saved the Canterbury settlement in economic terms. Wool exports doubled in value to £90,134 by 1858, and more than doubled again to £189,498 by 1860, providing the Provincial Council with revenue to spend on public works.

Christchurch was New Zealand's first city. Although it must have amused overseas visitors to be told that this scattered village of wooden shops and houses was a city, it was indeed so, from 1856, by virtue of a royal charter. This was achieved simply because it became the seat of an Anglican bishop. Canterbury's first bishop-designate, Dr Jackson, had arrived soon after the first main body of settlers, but returned to England after only six weeks. After some unseemly wrangling, the Reverend Henry John Chitty Harper was consecrated by the Archbishop of Canterbury, and arrived at Lyttelton with his growing family on 23 December 1856. He was an ideal choice for a new colony: practical, energetic, sincere and steadfast. The provincial period in Christchurch is hard to imagine without Bishop Harper, who consolidated the Anglican Church on a sound financial basis and succeeded in getting the Cathedral built.

The biggest issue of the early 1850s in Christchurch was how to get better access to Lyttelton. All heavy goods still had to risk the Sumner Bar before

Henry John Chitty Harper (1804–93), first Anglican Bishop of Christchurch (1856–90), and his wife Emily were key figures in the city's religious and social life. They had fifteen children in a long and happy marriage. Harper did much to set the Anglican Church in Canterbury on secure foundations, and to get the cathedral built.

CM 416C

Women of colonial Christchurch: from left, Fanny Beatty, Nina Gresson, Clarissa Gresson, Ellen Beatty, Ann Gresson, on 2 September 1867. Henry Barnes Gresson (1809–1901) was Provincial Solicitor, Crown Prosecutor and Judge for the South Island from 1857 to 1875. Mrs Gresson died in 1889.

Dr A. C. Barker photograph, CM 350

coming up the Avon or Heathcote Rivers, and many smaller boats overturned in the surf. The lawyer Henry Gresson lost all his luggage and family silver in a wreck in 1854. FitzGerald pushed for the completion of the Sumner Road via Evans Pass, started by Captain Thomas but still unfinished. Another faction urged a canal from the Estuary. (This idea had a remarkably long life in Christchurch.) After receiving two reports rejecting all other options, the Provincial Council in 1854 voted £10,000 to continue work on the Sumner Road. Rocky cliffs near the summit proved an expensive obstacle, however, and various solutions were suggested, including a tunnel near the top. The cheapest compromise won: a lower road-line and a zig-zag instead of a tunnel. On 24 August 1857 FitzGerald drove his dog-cart over the new road and all the way to Lyttelton,

The Christchurch Club, Latimer Square, 26 November 1861, looking south, with Collins' Hotel (later the Occidental) in the distance. This was New Zealand's first gentlemen's club, and gave early runholders a place to stay when visiting town.

Dr A. C. Barker photograph, CM 247/1

Alfred Charles Barker (1819–73). Christchurch's first doctor and registrar of births, deaths and marriages, he retired from medicine after his wife's death in 1858 and devoted his last years to his farms, his family and photography, leaving a valuable collection of glass-plate negatives to the Canterbury Museum.
CM

Detail from W. T. L. Travers' photograph of Ferrymead Wharf, 1863. The gabled Ferrymead Hotel (centre) still survives, though much altered. Nothing else is left, apart from some wharf piles. This was Christchurch's main port of entry for heavy goods until the opening of the Lyttelton rail tunnel.
Auckland Art Gallery/Toi o Tamaki

just before he ended his term as superintendent and set off for London as the province's immigration agent. Next month the first daily postal service commenced between Lyttelton and Christchurch, but the hazardous zig-zag deterred all except the bravest of carriers. The access problem between the city and its port remained acute.

Industrial development was slow before the advent of the railways in the 1860s and the surge in demand for agricultural machinery of the 1870s. Apart from Anderson's forge, Christchurch in 1857 could boast only a windmill, two watermills, three breweries, a printing office and a tree nursery. Over the next decade, however, small-scale workshops proliferated, making boots, wheels, barrels, rope, harnesses, and all the other hand-made local products of a typical mid-Victorian town. Aulsebrook's biscuit factory was established in 1863. Brick kilns made use of abundant clay deposits at the foot of the Port Hills, and the lower Heathcote River became a favoured site for tanneries and glue factories.

Assisted immigration had halted in 1853, but resumed in 1855 with financial assistance from Godley and Henry Selfe. Now the Canterbury Provincial Council could afford to assist immigrants and employ an agent in England. The peak of this first phase came in 1863–64, when over 6,000 new settlers came to Canterbury. The population of Christchurch accordingly more than doubled from about 3,000 in 1862 to 6,500 in 1866, perhaps the fastest period of growth in the city's entire history. It took another ten years to reach 12,000 in 1876.

FitzGerald's successor as superintendent was William Sefton Moorhouse (1857–63 and 1866–68), a charming man with progressive ideas who was sometimes as careless with public money as he was with his own. In a long and colourful career, his outstanding achievement was the construction of the rail tunnel linking Lyttelton to Christchurch. The Canterbury Pilgrims had left England during the great period of railway expansion, and some would have seen a tunnel as the obvious solution to the transport problem but far too expensive for such a small community. Yet the problem of access was desperate, and the sudden increase in value of Canterbury's exports between 1856 and 1858 convinced the Provincial Council that it could finance the work. In October 1858 Moorhouse announced the decision to build a tunnel. The cost was set at

Detail from Dr Barker's 1860 panorama of Christchurch. View towards the south-west, with Gloucester Street in the fore-ground and W. D. Wood's 1856 Antigua Street windmill in the distance. Note the sod wall in the foreground, wooden fences and well-built brick chimneys. These signs of progress contrast with surviving tussock, even on the streets.
CM 374

£235,000 and preliminary work started in 1860, but the English contractors gave up when they struck harder rock than expected.

FitzGerald returned from London to become the most outspoken critic of Moorhouse's rail-tunnel project, and what he called the 'Yankeeism' of the Provincial Council's public works programme. But FitzGerald's doubts were shared only by some runholders; for once, most of Christchurch was united behind Moorhouse. As a mouthpiece for his views and a rival to his former employer the *Lyttelton Times*, FitzGerald founded *The Press* in May 1861. Thus Christchurch acquired its two major newspapers.

Moorhouse soon found another tunnel contractor in Australia, whose men started work on the Heathcote portal in July 1861. Edward Dobson was the provincial engineer who supervised the work, and his skill was demonstrated when the two drives met exactly as planned in May 1867. The opening of the Lyttelton Tunnel on 9 December 1867 was rightly celebrated as the Canterbury settlement's greatest achievement thus far. This was the first tunnel in the world to be driven through the wall of an extinct volcano. It was New Zealand's first rail tunnel, and remained for many years its longest.

It is indicative of the Provincial Council's optimism that work started on the tunnel before Canterbury even had a railway. This lack was remedied in April 1863 with the arrival of *Pilgrim*, a broad-gauge locomotive from Melbourne. After helping to build the line from Ferrymead wharf to Christchurch, *Pilgrim* hauled New Zealand's first public passenger train on 1 December 1863. By the time this line was connected to the Lyttelton tunnel, railway construction had reached the Selwyn River, south of Christchurch, and a northern line to Rangiora was being surveyed. Christchurch now had no spare land at the centre, so the railway station had to be located alongside the South Belt (Moorhouse Avenue).

Several major consequences flowed from this decision. The newly formed (May 1863) Christchurch Gas and Coal Company promptly bought land for its gasworks virtually next door on Waltham Road. As the railway expanded, its workers settled south of the station to form the district (and later borough) of Sydenham. Proximity to the railway ensured that Christchurch's next phase of

William Sefton Moorhouse (1825–81), Canterbury's second superintendent (1857–63 and 1866–68) and vigorous advocate of a rail tunnel to link Christchurch to its port at Lyttelton. His statue is at the entrance to the Botanic Gardens on Rolleston Avenue.
CM 4941

29

Right: The portal of the Lyttelton rail tunnel during construction, in February 1867. Edward Dobson, Provincial Engineer, is the figure with the white top hat, centre right. The rail link made Lyttelton a suburb of Christchurch and became the economic lifeline of Canterbury Province.

D. L. Mundy photograph, CM 9200

Below: Pilgrim, New Zealand's first steam locomotive, arrived at Lyttelton from Australia on 27 April 1863, and was landed at Ferrymead on 6 May, to help construct the broad-gauge line to Christchurch.

CM

Christchurch's first town halls, on High Street between Cashel and Lichfield Streets, shown here in 1865. The smaller wooden hall was opened on 1 October 1857, but soon proved far too small. The much larger stone hall was completed in 1863, but was so badly damaged by an earthquake on 5 June 1869 that it was condemned. Strange's department store was later built on this site.

Dr A. C. Barker photograph, CM 1143

industrial development would take place in Woolston and Addington, and that Moorhouse Avenue would become lined with large stores for wool and grain.

Christchurch was gazetted a municipal district in February 1862, and at the first meeting of the Municipal Council next month John Hall was elected its first chairman. Besides approving Christchurch's first street lighting (sixty-two kerosene lamps in June 1862), this first council authorised the sinking of the city's first water well in February 1864; it gushed to a height of nearly four metres, demonstrating the existence of ample supplies of pure artesian water. The city's first meeting of ratepayers took place in February 1863. Thus the Provincial Council gradually began to yield the functions of local government to an elected borough council. But the town's revenue from rates was meagre compared with the province's large income from land sales, so development of civic amenities was painfully slow at first.

Steady growth of business in Christchurch during the boom years of 1857–64 was reflected in the appearance of yet more banks. The Bank of New South Wales opened its first Christchurch branch in 1861, and the Bank of New Zealand in 1862. They were followed by the Bank of Australasia in 1864. Two years later the BNZ moved to an impressive new classical building on the corner of Hereford and Colombo Streets, at the entrance to the Square, where it remained for nearly a century as one of the city's best-known landmarks. Another symptom of growth was the opening of New Zealand's first telegraph, between Christchurch and Lyttelton, in July 1863.

Christchurch's early newspapers aspired to high literary standards, and in April 1865 the first issue appeared of *Punch in Canterbury*, modelled on the famous English journal. While it lasted, this taught the Pilgrims to laugh at themselves in verse and cartoons. It was edited by a talented rhymster, Crosbie Ward, a wealthy young Anglo-Irishman who came out in 1852 after his two elder brothers were

John Hall (1824–1907), sheep farmer, politician and Premier of New Zealand 1879–82. He was resident magistrate and first chairman of Christchurch's Town Board (1862–63). As Sir John Hall, he was again Mayor of Christchurch in 1906.

CM 14043

31

Christchurch's first classical building, the Bank of New Zealand on the corner of Colombo and Hereford Streets. Designed by Melbourne architect Leonard Terry and completed in 1866, it was demolished in 1963, perhaps the saddest loss of all the city's historic buildings.

Dr A. C. Barker photograph, CM 3781

Benjamin Woolfield Mountfort (1825–98) designed many of Canterbury's early wooden churches and the Provincial Council Buildings. The stone Council Chamber (1865) is his masterpiece, but he also designed the Museum and Canterbury College's clock tower and Great Hall. Mountfort was the leading exponent of Gothic Revival architecture in nineteenth-century New Zealand.

CM 5279

drowned near Quail Island in Lyttleton Harbour. With Christopher Bowen, he bought the *Lyttelton Times* in 1856 for £5,000. Crosbie's 1858 'Song of the Squatters', a witty comment on the land-regulations debate, became a Canterbury classic. One of the Christchurch Club's visitors in the 1860s was the English novelist Samuel Butler, who wrote for *The Press* while farming at Mesopotamia in the upper Rangitata Valley. His New Zealand experiences formed part of the inspiration for his novel *Erewhon*. With the likes of Butler and Crosbie Ward, Canterbury was a literary as well as aristocratic province in the 1860s.

Christchurch in the 1850s and 1860s was a frontier town in more than just appearance. Crime was not a serious problem, apart from petty theft, but the clergy denounced drunkenness and prostitution as major social evils. Christchurch had numerous grog shops and no fewer than twenty-eight known brothels in 1869. The city was scandalised to discover that one of its police constables, Martin Cash, was running a bevy of brothels. He was in fact a Tasmanian bushranger on the run, and now fled to Otago.

Canterbury's seven fat years were followed by six years of lean stagnation (1865–71), during which trade declined, wool prices fell and newly arrived immigrants found it hard to get work. The discovery of gold on the West Coast in 1865 was partly to blame, as it caused another exodus of young males. Yet the city was steadily acquiring the amenities of civilised society. Christchurch Hospital opened in 1862, and the city's doctors formed New Zealand's first medical association in 1865. The first horticultural society was formed in 1861, and the Canterbury Agricultural and Pastoral Association held its first show in 1863.

John Robert Godley died in England on 28 October 1861. The news of his death caused much sadness in Christchurch, as many of the Pilgrims still regarded him fondly as the leader and founder of the Canterbury settlement. A year later, a citizens' meeting decided to erect a statue of him in Cathedral Square. The unveiling of the Godley statue (New Zealand's first public statue) in August 1867 was a great occasion in Christchurch, and a reunion for those who had arrived on the First Four Ships. On the plinth Godley was described as

'Founder of Canterbury', though this title ought really to be shared with Edward Gibbon Wakefield, who had died in Wellington in May 1862.

Soon after the opening of the rail tunnel, Lord Lyttelton arrived in January 1868 to inspect the colony he had helped to launch. He was taken by special train to Christchurch, where a civic reception and dinner awaited him. (This was the first sign that the tunnel had made Lyttelton a suburb of Christchurch. Even the Customs Department moved to Christchurch in 1869.) Lord Lyttelton declared himself suitably impressed by the colonists' efforts but was sorry that the Cathedral had not progressed beyond the level of its foundations. Of Christchurch, he declared that he 'had seen a town, certainly the most curious he had

Mountfort's masterpiece, the Canterbury Provincial Council Buildings, nearing completion in 1865. Gloucester Street in the foreground. The stone debating chamber on the right contains the finest surviving Gothic Revival interior in New Zealand.

J. Elsbee photograph, CM 4966

Charles Christopher Bowen (1830–1917), poet, educator, magistrate, administrator and politician. He arrived on the *Charlotte Jane* in 1850 and was Godley's secretary before becoming Provincial Treasurer, Minister of Justice and later Speaker of the House of Representatives.

CM 9319

Unveiling the Godley statue, Cathedral Square, 6 August 1867. C. C. Bowen in a black top hat is the speaker. Dr Barker's house in the background is today the site of the AMP building.

Dr A. C. Barker photograph, CM 4852

Plan
OF THE
CITY OF CHRISTCHURCH
Canterbury, N.Z.
1868

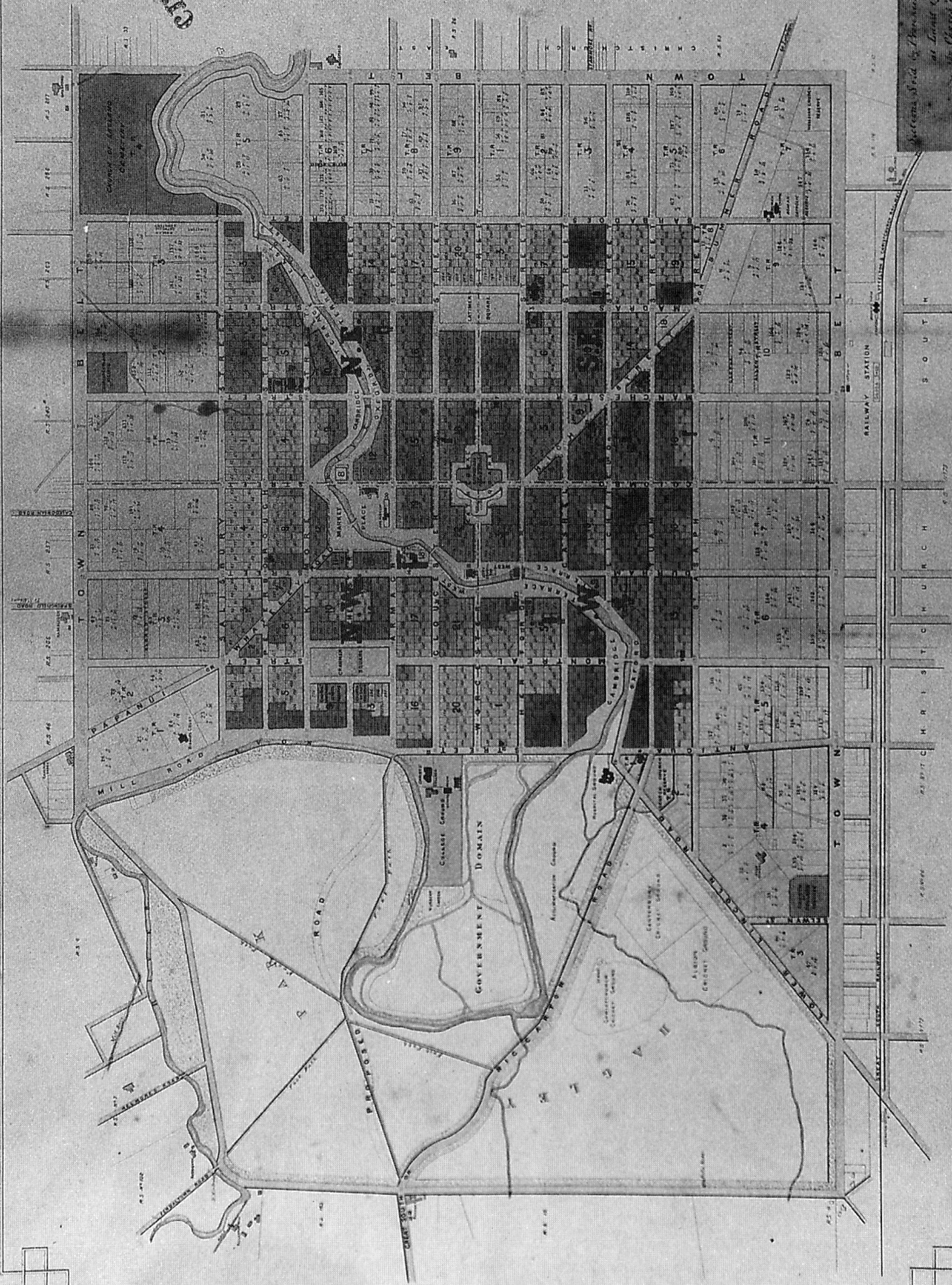

ever seen, a town and not a town, which had been laid out on so large a scale, that it held out a prospect of being of considerable magnitude . . .'

The banquet for Lord Lyttelton took place in the town's worst week so far. Early in February Canterbury was visited by its most severe storm since the start of European settlement. Ships were wrecked in Lyttelton Harbour, and the heavy rain caused surface flooding in many places. Most serious of all, the Waimakariri River burst its banks and flowed into its ancient channels on the northwest side of Christchurch. Much of the water came down the Avon, and flowed a metre deep across the Market Place (now Victoria Square). Many shops and houses were damaged by floodwaters and silt deposits. In February 1869 the South Waimakariri River Board was set up to devise the best means to protect Christchurch against further serious flooding, the first of many efforts in this direction. But it took another sixty years to bring the river under effective control.

William Rolleston became Canterbury's last superintendent in May 1868. (Samuel Bealey had served one term from 1863, and William Moorhouse had been returned in 1866 for a fourth term.) Although Moorhouse is remembered as the superintendent who got things done, Rolleston was the more admired in his day as the reliable administrator; honest, prudent and 'sound'. As other provinces

William Wilson (1819–97), first Mayor of Christchurch, 1868. Also known as 'Cabbage' Wilson, from his extensive market gardens.
CM 9031

Left: 'Breakfast to Lord Lyttelton', 1868. The scene in Christchurch's second Town Hall, High Street, when the Canterbury Pilgrims welcomed the former chairman of the Canterbury Association. This is the earliest surviving indoor photograph of a public gathering in Christchurch, if not in New Zealand.

H. Gourlay photograph, CM

Opposite: W. Dartnell's 1868 map of Christchurch.

CM 14472

declined in the 1870s, 'Canterbury stood out as the model province and Rolleston as the model superintendent'. His early interest in education never waned, and with his friend Christopher Bowen he made the 1864 Canterbury system of public schools the model for the whole of New Zealand in the 1877 Education Act.

Economic prospects brightened in the late 1860s, stimulated by the opening of the Lyttelton tunnel and improvements at the port. Then the recovery turned into a boom in the early 1870s. Wool prices improved and the spread of small farming on the plains dramatically increased grain production. The railway now gave farmers easy access to Lyttelton, where clipper ships called in ever-increasing numbers to carry away Canterbury's wool and wheat. In 1877 one of these, the *Crusader*, reduced the voyage between New Zealand and England to sixty-five days. Rather than be at the behest of British shippers, a group of leading Christchurch businessmen launched the New Zealand Shipping Company in 1873. Provincial Council revenue, which had slumped since 1868, now rebounded and exceeded £1 million for the first time in 1874. Wool exports likewise passed the £1 million mark in 1875. Flushed with prosperity, the city's lawyers and businessmen founded their own Canterbury Club in 1874, to rival the runholders' Christchurch Club, and built on the corner of Cambridge Terrace and Worcester Street.

Helping to turn recovery into boom were the expansionist policies of central government announced by Julius Vogel in 1870. Massive loans financed a rapid expansion in public works, especially railways, while government-assisted immigration provided the necessary labour force. This scheme brought a flood

The Great Flood of 4 February 1868. This is the Gloucester Street footbridge to the Provincial Council Buildings, already largely obscured by trees. The street lamp on the right was one of the city council's second batch of gas lamps, replacing earlier kerosene lamps.

D. L. Mundy photograph, CM 1401/8

Above: Durham Street Methodist Church, which opened on Christmas Day, 1864. This is the earliest-known photograph (probably taken soon after completion) of the first stone church on the Canterbury Plains, and the city's earliest Gothic Revival stone building.

Brittenden Collection, CHAC/CM

Below: The second Victoria Street bridge, 1865. Probably the earliest iron-and-stone bridge in New Zealand, it is now preserved as the James Hay Bridge in Victoria Square.

Dr A. C. Barker photograph, CM 41

of new immigrants to Canterbury, nearly twenty thousand between 1871 and 1876. Over a third of the single women were Irish, and one ship in 1872 brought several hundred Germans, Poles and Scandinavians. Land sales boomed, as many of the new arrivals intended to become farmers. Speculators made fortunes from the subdivision of cheap rural land, until the boom collapsed in 1878. The immigrants of the seventies changed the composition of Christchurch's population decisively, ending its early, mainly English and Anglican, character. Yet this more cosmopolitan population also enhanced the pride of the pioneers, especially those who had climbed the Bridle Path before the rail tunnel was opened.

These new arrivals found Christchurch a small town that was at long last beginning to shake off the raw 'Wild West' look of its early days, with many new buildings in brick or stone as well as wood. The Canterbury Museum (1870) was the first significant public building in what became the city's cultural and educational precinct, near Christ's College. Canterbury (University) College moved into its first permanent buildings opposite the Museum in 1877, sharing the block with the new Christchurch Boys' High School, designed in a similar Gothic Revival style. Not far away, at the northern end of Cranmer Square, the Normal School (opened in April 1876) became New Zealand's first teachers' training college in 1877.

Another sign of increasing maturity and prosperity was the rebuilding of earlier wooden churches in stone during the early 1870s. Visitors remarked on the prominence of churches in the townscape, and for a while Christchurch was known as the 'City of Churches'. The first stone churches were St John the Baptist's, in Latimer Square, and the Durham Street Methodist Church, both completed in 1864. Benjamin Mountfort was the architect for the Trinity Congregational Church (1874) and Holy Trinity, Avonside (1876), which bear strong resemblances to his Canterbury Museum and College buildings. St Peter's, Upper Riccarton, began its long rebuilding in stone in the 1870s. But some significant wooden churches in Christchurch also date from this period, such as St Michael and All Angels' (1872) and St Paul's, Papanui (1876–77). The Roman Catholic Pro-Cathedral, built in Barbadoes Street in 1864 with lower walls of stone and wood above, was now enlarged with the addition of gabled side aisles.

Yet Canterbury's capital still lacked its cathedral. The foundation stone had been laid in December 1864 and the foundations completed by the end of 1865, but then funds ran out and work was suspended. Some thought the diocese had more urgent things to spend its money on, and a proposal to sell the Cathedral site was only narrowly defeated in the 1869 Anglican Synod. The novelist Anthony Trollope, visiting Christchurch in 1872, was saddened by the sight of the weed-infested foundations. He was told the Cathedral might never be built.

It was Bishop Harper's fine example in pledging £50 a year from his modest salary which finally prodded the Anglican elite of Canterbury to get on with building the Christchurch Cathedral. Several leading citizens pledged substantial support, and building resumed in 1873, with Mountfort as supervising architect. He proposed extensive alterations to Sir Gilbert Scott's plans, but the Rhodes family (who donated the tower, spire and most of the bells) insisted on the original design. The nave and tower were finished by 1881. The chancel and transepts were not completed until 1904 (by which time Mountfort

'The Great Fire of Lyttelton' (24 October 1870) started in some straw-filled packing cases and ran out of control before the fire brigade could reach it. The business heart of the port was completely destroyed, with insured losses of £80,000. It was New Zealand's most expensive fire to that date.

CM 3446

The Canterbury Club (established 1874) was the merchants' rival to the Christchurch Club, and still has a membership largely comprising lawyers, accountants and businessmen.

Brittenden Collection, CHAC/CM

had added a west porch of his own design in 1894), but from the 1880s Christchurch at last had its architectural centrepiece, and was known thereafter as New Zealand's 'Cathedral City'.

From the early 1850s a significant number of Pilgrims chose to live on their rural sections rather than in town. Successful businessmen and a few professionals built large wooden houses where they could enjoy a gentlemanly lifestyle. These were the precursors of Christchurch's residential suburbs. By the late 1870s there were almost as many people living in the suburbs as resided within the inner city.

St Albans took its name from George Dickinson's farm (his actress cousin had become the Duchess of St Albans). Although much of the land was peat or swamp, dairy farms and market gardens did well here. Many of the early householders were Wesleyans, and the Methodist church in St Albans Lane (1859) was the district's first public building. Papanui was one of Christchurch's earliest suburbs because of its patch of forest, which soon disappeared to build the city. Merivale became a fashionable suburb from the 1860s, but Fendalton was much slower to develop. (Its original name, Fendall's Town, must have been a joke, for there was no sign of any town, just fields and deep creeks.) Upper Riccarton grew quickly around St Peter's (1858), a little wooden church located in the fork between the main roads south and west, where blacksmiths and harness-makers served Riccarton Racecourse.

On the eastern side of town, Avonside and Linwood attracted early settlers, mainly because so many of the Pilgrims liked the look of the land as they came up the Avon River towards Christchurch. Ferry Road was a major artery of the city's transport pattern throughout the nineteenth century, with shops and houses dotted along its entire length. The wharf at Radley on the Heathcote River was a busy spot for early shipping. Woolston also developed quickly around the cob church of St John (1857) on Ferry Road. Nearby, tanneries and wool-scouring industries lined the Heathcote River, but the southern residential suburbs of Opawa, St Martins and Beckenham remained largely rural in appearance until the 1900s.

Sydenham was originally part of W. S. Moorhouse's farm 'Spreydon', but it was very swampy in the 1850s, with sheets of surface water after rain. Its earliest settlers in the 1860s were Lancashire immigrants, so that the district was at first known as 'Lanky-town'. Most were labourers or small tradesmen who worked in the city but could not afford city land prices. The 1860s saw rapid subdivision and the growth of a railway town, called Sydenham after a South London suburb. Little wooden cottages clustered more densely here than in any other part of Christchurch. A large school was built in 1873 in semi-ecclesiastical style, with a tower and steeple that still outdid St Saviour's Church when it was built opposite. Sydenham was Christchurch's first borough (1877) outside the inner city. By then it had a population of 6,500 – half the size of Christchurch City, and equal to all the other suburbs combined. It was already developing its own distinctive character: radical, dissenting and working class, a heartland of left-wing politics in New Zealand.

Christchurch grew rapidly in the early 1870s, perhaps too rapidly for its own good, as the provincial era ended with serious public health problems. Epidemics of diphtheria and whooping cough were annual events from 1872 to 1875,

John Ollivier (1812–93), publisher, magistrate, philanthropist and political organiser for Moorhouse and Bealey. The 'king-maker' of Canterbury provincial politics, he was a hearty, jolly man, intensely energetic, ready to take the lead in any good cause. Alfred Cox said of Ollivier that he 'never made an enemy, never lost a friend'.

CM 14908

Opposite top: The Normal School, Cranmer Square, soon after its opening in April 1876. (The goalposts suggest that the crowd is watching a football match.) This became New Zealand's first teachers' training college in 1877. One of Christchurch's most important Gothic Revival buildings, it has recently been converted to apartments.

E. R. Webb Collection, CM 5433

Opposite bottom: Julius von Haast contemplating some of the moa skeletons that made the Canterbury Museum world famous in the 1870s. A swamp at Glenmark in North Canterbury yielded such an abundance of bones that he was able to exchange moa skeletons with leading European museums for their surplus exhibits.

Dr A. C. Barker photograph, CM 109

and the typhoid epidemic of 1875–76 claimed the lives of 152 citizens. Christchurch had become notorious as New Zealand's 'fever capital', with much higher mortality rates from diphtheria, typhoid and scarlet fever than the other main centres. Citizens wondered why the city was so unhealthy.

The answer lay at their feet. Despite the abundance of pure artesian water, Christchurch in 1876 was a remarkably smelly city, and this was not just from the polluted Avon River into which the hospital and assorted breweries discharged their waste. The side channels of many inner-city streets were choked with 'slops', which in those days included the contents of chamber pots as well as kitchen waste. Wells for drinking water were frequently contaminated by nearby cesspits. The unpaved streets were always littered with manure from horses and, from 1874, animals being driven to the saleyards in Deans Avenue. The City Council had seen the need for proper drainage in the early sixties, and ordered a large shipment of iron pipes from England, but by the time they arrived the council was nearly bankrupt and had to sell them off, so the city stayed soggy.

The provincial period came to an end in November 1876, with the abolition of the provincial councils and their replacement by numerous town boards, boroughs, road boards and harbour boards throughout New Zealand. Canterbury had been one of the most successful of the provinces, prospering from wool and wheat, and spared the disruption caused in the North Island by the

Shops in Victoria Street, between Kilmore and Peterborough Streets, in the 1870s. The enterprising Mr Woodard ('Boots made to order . . . pegged, sewed and riveted') would not have been out of place on the American Wild West, but the whole scene is also reminiscent of an English provincial town of the mid-Victorian era.

CM 4333

42

Above: Christchurch Railway Station, 1872, showing the broad-gauge tracks and early four-wheel carriages. The locomotive is probably No. 4, one of the second group of 0-4-2T locomotives imported from Australia. The gauge was changed to New Zealand standard narrow gauge in 1876, and a new Gothic-style railway station was completed in 1877.

Weekly Press photograph, 2 August 1905, Canterbury Museum

Below: Lyttelton in 1875, before completion of the Timeball Station, showing the extent of reclamation with spoil from the rail tunnel. The original shoreline was a little to the left of the flagpole in the foreground.

Pilgrims' Association Collection, CM 2130

Market day in Cathedral Square, 28 May 1871. The future Post Office site is in the foreground. The gabled structure at left is the Torlesse Building (1864), designed by Maxwell Bury. It survived until 1916.

Dr A. C. Barker photograph, CM/ACB 73-1/2

Land Wars, or New Zealand Wars, of the 1860s. Indeed, Maori faces were rarely seen in Christchurch in the late nineteenth century. Loss of land, and the scourge of European diseases, had marginalised Ngai Tahu.

Canterbury's capital and its immediate suburbs now contained nearly half of the province's people. By 1876 there were 12,815 people living in the central city, and an estimated ten thousand in the surrounding suburbs. Lyttelton, with just 3,224 inhabitants, had long since been overshadowed by the sprawling cathedral city on the plains. Apart from its death rate, Christchurch was no longer a frontier town.

CHAPTER THREE

Victorian City

1877 – 1902

In this period Christchurch endured a long economic depression, which was more severe in Canterbury than in the rest of New Zealand, but it then recovered sooner and more strongly than most other places in the 1890s. Its prosperity was still closely tied to the exports of Canterbury's farmers, and most of the city's major industries either served the farming sector or processed its products. The city matured remarkably in the 1880s and 1890s, with many elegant commercial and public buildings, while spreading suburbs of wooden villas were linked to the central city by a steam- and horse-drawn tramway network. Christchurch led New Zealand in many fields in this period: in its drainage and sanitation reforms, in women's suffrage and the temperance movement, in the growth of trade unions and radical politics, in education and in sport. It was also home to some colourful eccentrics and several small religious sects, which encouraged North Islanders to make jokes about 'Barmy Christchurch' when they weren't calling it the 'City of Cycles'. The way most cyclists rode wherever they liked made both nicknames seem perfectly apt.

Victorian Christchurch: solid, respectable and sunny, but struggling with the 'Long Depression'. View south-west from the Cathedral tower, 1885. The Torlesse Building is now dwarfed by the New Zealand Insurance Company building (1885) and the Post Office (1879). The latter, designed by P. F. M. Burrows in Venetian Gothic, is one of the city's most important nineteenth-century public buildings.

F. A. Coxhead photograph, CM 182

George Gould (1823–89), born at Hambleden on the River Thames, came to Christchurch in 1851. His store in Armagh Street was the second wooden building erected in Christchurch, after the Land Office. He was an energetic and enterprising businessman who made a fortune shipping wool and wheat, and was a great benefactor of early Christchurch until worsening deafness excluded him from public life.

CM 16207

Victorian Christchurch was like a far-flung fragment of Victorian England. After making allowances for the smaller population (about 44,000 by 1886), and the relative newness of its streets and buildings, a visitor to Christchurch from Norwich or Nottingham in the 1880s would have recognised many familiar institutions. As we have seen, there were plenty of churches. Now there was a cathedral, a fine museum and botanic gardens, a university college, a mechanics' institute and a public library. It was a community suffused with Victorian values of self-reliance and self-improvement. Christchurch was full of voluntary associations, from lodges and friendly societies to brass bands and the fire brigade. And just as Victorian England experienced the 'games revolution', so too Christchurch could claim by the 1890s to be New Zealand's sporting capital. Yet the façade of Victorian success and respectability sometimes barely concealed an economic reality of uncertainty, unemployment and hardship for many ordinary people.

Vogel's expansionist policies led to a land boom in Canterbury in 1877. With the demise of the provincial government, more than a million acres of Crown land were released for railway development and farming. Rich individuals and companies bought land cheaply, subdivided it and sold it on, often at great profit. There was such strong demand from men who wanted to buy smaller farms to share in the wheat bonanza that speculators could push prices upwards. The bubble burst quite suddenly in November 1878, leaving many with heavy debts and over-valued farms. Worse was to come. Falling wool and wheat prices worldwide plunged Australia and New Zealand into recession in 1879, which then deepened into the 'Long Depression' of the 1880s.

'Cabstand Corner' in the early 1880s (later known as 'The Triangle'). High Street on the left, Colombo Street on the right, Port Hills in the distance, horse-drawn tram No. 8 on Colombo Street. A decade later this scene would be full of people on bicycles.

E. Wheeler & Son photograph, CM 15829

Left: Christchurch Cathedral under construction, 1878. View north towards Colombo Street. The Cathedral was consecrated on 1 November 1881, with tower and spire but only half the nave. It was finally completed in 1904.

F. Wheeler & Son photograph. A. Selwyn Bruce Collection, CM 8732

Below: View south from the Cathedral tower, 1882, looking down Colombo Street towards Cashmere Hill. Bank of New Zealand in centre foreground.

F .A. Coxhead photograph, CM 2214

Above: View east from Chester Street Fire Station tower, c. 1880, showing the Oxford Terrace/Manchester Street intersection. The thickly wooded area to the left is now the site of the Edmonds Band Rotunda.

Stansell collection, CHAC/CM61

Below: View north from Cathedral tower, c. 1880, looking along Colombo Street. The large barn-like building in Market Square was the Market Hall and Christchurch's first post office. The Chester Street Fire Station is visible centre right, identified by its narrow tower.

Burton Brothers photograph, CM 2883

Christchurch's prosperity was so heavily dependent on Canterbury's farmers that the city could not escape these blows. Assisted immigration continued into the early 1880s, but the exodus was greater: every year between 1883 and 1887 more people left Canterbury than arrived from Britain. Unemployment became a serious social problem well into the 1890s. Yet this remains one of the great wheat-producing periods in Canterbury's history. Demand for wheat enabled small farmers to survive on the land, even when prices were low, because more than half of the crop was consumed within New Zealand (three-quarters in 1884). The value of grain exports was sometimes almost half that of wool, and actually exceeded it in 1880 and 1883.

Wool remained the sheet anchor of Canterbury's overseas trade, but what helped the province to weather the depression most of all was the advent of refrigeration. The Canterbury Frozen Meat Company was incorporated in 1882, and the Belfast Freezing Works began operation in February 1883. The first shipment of frozen mutton from Lyttelton was arranged by the Christchurch-based New Zealand Shipping Company on the *British King* in April 1883. In London it soon became famous as 'Canterbury lamb'. Lyttelton was at last becoming a port rather than just a harbour, with new jetties and cranes and further reclamation.

While the main source of Canterbury's prosperity lay in its exports of wool, wheat and meat, Christchurch developed a strong secondary-industries sector in this period. Even during the depths of the 1880s depression, new factories and businesses were still being established and, as economic conditions improved in the late 1890s, some enjoyed spectacular success from exporting their products. The old-established foundries of Anderson's and Scott's were now among New Zealand's largest, making heavy machinery, locomotives and bridges. Most other Christchurch factories used local raw materials. The Kaiapoi Woollen Mills Company employed 475 in its Cashel Street clothing factory in the

Aulsebrook's biscuit factory, 1880s. Probably the company's second premises, after their move to the Montreal/St Asaph Street corner in 1879.

CM 5567

Above: Addington Railway Workshops, soon after completion of the water tower (1883), one of New Zealand's earliest reinforced concrete structures. The workshops became one of the city's biggest employers in the late nineteenth century, and produced New Zealand's first locally designed steam locomotive (W192) in 1889.

French collection, CHAC/CM 931

Below: Hereford Street, looking east from Oxford Terrace, 1880. On the far left is the Bank of New South Wales (1867), designed by Dunedin architects Mason and Clayton, and one of the city's earliest commercial buildings in stone. At centre is the wooden Shand's Building (1851), now the oldest surviving commercial building in Christchurch.

Wheeler photograph, CM 3363

1880s, and the Tai Tapu Dairy Company moved to Addington in 1892: its Fernleaf butter brand soon became as famous in Britain as Canterbury lamb.

By 1896 the great majority of Christchurch's factory workers were employed in freezing works, tanneries, footwear, clothing, and printing and publishing. For a few years near the turn of the century, Christchurch may have been the industrial capital of New Zealand, just ahead of Auckland in both numbers of workers (if one includes Belfast and Kaiapoi) and value of production. But it was a brief moment: Auckland then outstripped every other centre and began its twentieth-century rise to dominance in the New Zealand economy.

Christchurch had been New Zealand's unhealthiest city in the 1870s, but in the 1880s it became the first New Zealand city to have a proper underground sewerage system. The new Christchurch Drainage Board, which first met on 4 January 1876, had relatively wide powers for the time, and covered almost all of what became the metropolitan area. One of its first acts was to commission a system of permanent sewers to drain the central city. Rainwater would be channelled into streams and rivers, while sewage and household waste were kept separate and carried into large brick underground sewers, which converged at the Tuam Street/Fitzgerald Avenue intersection. A pumping station in Linwood then pumped the sewage out to the sandhills of Bromley to New Zealand's first 'sewage farm', where the filtered and treated sewage fertilised the pastures of the board's model farm. Construction began in 1879, and pumping commenced in September 1882. When work stopped in 1884, Christchurch had 36 miles of sewers, but only 639 houses were connected.

Worcester Street in the 1890s, looking towards the Canterbury Museum, which then had a spire (or flèche). The Clock Tower on the left was the first of Mountfort's buildings for Canterbury University College (1877–79). The Great Hall, beyond it, was completed in 1882.
CM 3077

The Drainage Board had also decided to accept responsibility as a local board of health under the 1876 Health Act (it was the only one in New Zealand before 1900). Dr Courtney Nedwill, its second medical officer, was a tireless campaigner for sanitary reform who declared war on cesspits. There were at least a thousand of these in the central city in 1876, but by 1882 they had all been closed and replaced by pan closets. The new sewers helped indirectly, because ground water seeped into the system through the pipe joints and significantly lowered the water table, making the city a drier and healthier place than before. The elimination of cesspits largely solved the typhoid problem, and the effect on the city's death rate was dramatic: from an appalling 30 per thousand in 1875, the rate was almost halved by 1881 (before the sewers came into use), and halved again to 9.5 per thousand in 1889, close to the twentieth-century average.

Even so, by modern standards Christchurch in the 1880s was not a very salubrious town. Horse droppings bred clouds of flies in hot weather, and mingled with the dust that plagued Christchurch whenever the nor'westers blew. An Englishwoman, 'Hopeful', disgusted by the flies she saw in butchers' and fruiterers' shops, returned 'Home' to publish her adverse impressions under the title *Taken In* (1887). She complained of Christchurch's 'hot, stony, dusty, noisy streets' and its 'filthy degraded-looking back yards'. Most of the houses she thought 'squalid', but conceded that there were some 'pretty little gardens attached to the most humble shanties'. Other visitors were alarmed by the

Opening of the season at the Canterbury Rowing Club, 1893; view north from Ward's Brewery, on the corner of Kilmore Street and Fitzgerald Avenue. Beyond are the boathouses of the Avon and Union clubs. Rowing and cycling were among Christchurch's most popular sports in the 1890s.

Hayward collection, CM 2358

'typhoid-laden stink' from side channels, and thought there were too many hotels and too much drinking.

In 1878 Christchurch had only five dentists and five chemists' shops, but forty-one hotels and six breweries: drunkenness was still a big social problem, in which women and children were the main losers. Several small, church-based abstinence societies had existed since the 1860s, but Christchurch became the main centre for the temperance movement in New Zealand in the 1880s and 1890s. By 1884 the city had over twenty temperance societies. They saw strength in unity, and formed the Women's Christian Temperance Union (WCTU) in 1885. The temperance movement had its headquarters in Sydenham, and two dynamic leaders, the Reverend L. M. Isitt and T. E. ('Tommy') Taylor, established the Sydenham Prohibition League in 1889. From 1890 their journal *The Prohibitionist* circulated widely throughout New Zealand.

Another hot issue was women's suffrage, which had close links with the temperance movement. Again, Christchurch led New Zealand in this campaign. Kate Sheppard, a pioneering Christchurch feminist, took charge of the WCTU's suffrage campaign in 1887, and presented the first of five suffrage petitions the following year. The final petition was signed by almost a third of the country's adult females. With support from Sir John Hall, one of Canterbury's veteran politicians, New Zealand women won the right to vote in 1893, the first to do so in the British Empire. Kate Sheppard also edited the WCTU's Christchurch-based journal, *The White Ribbon*.

Christchurch was the cradle of trade unions and artisan radicalism in New Zealand in this period. More specifically, Sydenham, 'the model borough', led the way. In the early 1880s a Working Men's Political Association was formed, critical of the 'polite' liberalism represented by the *Lyttelton Times*. Unemployment gave a sharp edge to their ideas and spurred the formation of unions. The Canterbury Labour Union (1887) and the Canterbury Trades and Labour Council (1890) were the most prominent of these. Unionists in Christchurch largely supported the Maritime Strike of 1890.

The general election of 1890 was the first one-man, one-vote election in New Zealand, and was greatly influenced by the recent industrial troubles. The Trades Council endorsed the Liberal Party's candidates in Christchurch electorates, all of whom were successful. Thus Christchurch became a Liberal stronghold for the next twenty years, in striking contrast to the conservatism of its social elite. One of these Liberal members, William Pember Reeves (son of the *Lyttelton Times* editor), became Christchurch's most famous reforming politician as a member of Seddon's government in the 1890s. He devised New Zealand's much-admired Industrial Conciliation and Arbitration Act (1894) and is regarded by some as the architect of state socialism in New Zealand. His *Ao-tea-Roa: The Long White Cloud* (1898) was an influential history which portrayed New Zealand as a 'progressive' society.

Christchurch in the 1890s seems to have been an exciting place, buzzing with new ideas, full of radicals, reformers and eccentrics. The city's most famous eccentric was also one of its most brilliant. Alexander Bickerton was Canterbury College's foundation Professor of Chemistry in 1874, and constantly challenged conventional views. His communitarian ideas led him to set up an experiment in communal living among the sandhills at Wainoni in 1896, and to criticise

Kate Sheppard (1848–1934) came to New Zealand in 1869 and was active in the Women's Christian Temperance Union before taking charge of its campaign for women's suffrage. Five petitions were presented, finally succeeding in 1893. New Zealand women were the first in the British Empire to get the vote. Sheppard was also a key figure in setting up the National Council of Women in 1896.
CM 90a

William Pember Reeves (1857–1932), one of New Zealand's outstanding politicians, reformers and writers. His 1894 Industrial Conciliation and Arbitration Act was a cornerstone of Liberal reforms. He was New Zealand's Agent-General in London from 1896, and Director of the London School of Economics 1908–19.
CM 11162

Right: Intersection of Papanui, Harewood and Main North roads, in the 1880s. We shall trace the changing appearance of this intersection across the next few decades as an example of suburban growth. Jackson's butchery with its two chimneys (right) was a local landmark. Beyond it is the two-storeyed Papanui Hotel, near the railway station.

Burton brothers photograph, CM 11704

Below: Christchurch Cathedral viewed across the new Gloucester Street bridge (1886) from the Provincial Council Buildings. The little shop on the corner (newly roofed in corrugated iron) had been there since the 1860s, when it was occupied by 'Gingerpop Raine', a manufacturer of lemonade and soda water. This site was later occupied by Maling's, the wine and spirit merchants.

CM 430/1

the institution of marriage, while his anti-imperialist views led him to oppose the South African war in 1899.

Bickerton's most brilliant student became one of New Zealand's world-famous sons. Ernest Rutherford came to Canterbury College from Nelson in 1890, and by 1893 had gained an MA with double first-class honours in mathematics and physics. With Bickerton's help, he also became an accomplished and original researcher. His first published paper, in 1894, was based on high-frequency electrical experiments conducted in a basement beside the Great Hall. Awarded the country's only science scholarship for overseas study, he left in 1895 to work in the Cavendish Laboratory at Cambridge University. Rutherford returned to Christchurch in 1900 to marry May Newton, his landlady's daughter, and then went on to win a Nobel Prize in 1908 for his work on radioactivity. In 1911 he discovered the nuclear model of the atom, thus becoming the father of nuclear science and one of the world's greatest scientists.

Most of Christchurch's citizens in this period were more interested in sport than science. Canterbury formed New Zealand's first rugby union, in 1879, and took a leading role in the game's administration. Lancaster Park, opened as a private venture in 1881, became the home of Canterbury rugby, and the No.1 Stand (1882) looked down on many notable matches for the next eighty years. In summer Lancaster Park was also the home of cricket in Canterbury. The New Zealand Cricket Council was formed in Christchurch in December 1894, and Canterbury has ever since dominated the administration of this sport.

Alexander William Bickerton (1842–1929), foundation Professor of Chemistry at Canterbury College in 1874, also taught physics and developed a theory of 'partial impact' to explain the origin of new stars. An unconventional and popular lecturer, he had a long dispute with the college authorities and was finally dismissed in 1902.

CM 7518

Cricket at Lancaster Park, 1895: Canterbury playing New South Wales. Beyond is the railway crossing on Wilsons Road, with a cluster of houses marking the intersection of Opawa and Shakespeare Roads. Waltham and Opawa were then thickly wooded and desirable suburbs.

Kinsey collection, CM 8912

Helen Connon (1859–1903), first woman student at Canterbury College and first woman in the British Empire to gain an honours degree (1881). She finally married her teacher, Professor John Macmillan Brown (after making him wait seven years), and was an outstanding headmistress of Christchurch Girls' High School.

CM 13100

Christchurch can claim to be the birthplace of several New Zealand sporting codes. Both the New Zealand Boxing and Hockey Associations were formed in Christchurch in 1902. It was certainly 'the cradle of tennis' in New Zealand. The Christchurch Lawn Tennis Club was founded in 1881, and at least eight clubs were active in the city by 1886. Bowls and croquet were also early starters in Christchurch, with several clubs flourishing in the 1880s, but they were late to organise nationally. Christchurch's flatness made the city ideal for cycling, and the Pioneer Bicycle Club (1870) was probably the first in New Zealand.

By the 1870s Christchurch had become New Zealand's leading centre for horse racing and training. Riccarton Racecourse was known throughout the country as the home of the New Zealand Cup and the Grand National Steeplechase. George Gatonby Stead and Sir George Clifford were leading importers and breeders who in 1896 helped set up the New Zealand Racing Conference, which was based in Christchurch until 1930. Cup Day was held in early November, to coincide with the A&P Show.

This combination created one of Christchurch's most distinctive institutions: Show Week. After the Showgrounds moved to Addington in 1887, the festival became known as 'Carnival Week', because of all the other events and entertainments it attracted. Hotels and boarding houses were always full in early November, when town and country came together. For over a century, Show Week at Addington was also a national institution, often attended by the Governor-General and leading politicians. Show Week acquired its third big attraction in 1899, when the New Zealand Metropolitan Trotting Club opened its new raceway next to the Showgrounds. Christchurch now became the headquarters of harness racing in New Zealand.

An American visitor in 1890 remarked that Christchurch was a city of 'bicycles, bridges and parsons'. By 1881 the city had no fewer than twenty-four different religious denominations meeting regularly. The Church of England was still nominally the largest of these, but low church attendances may have given the visitor an impression of more parsons than parishioners. Even so, the churches played an important role in charitable aid to the poor in pre-welfare-state days, as did the numerous lodges and friendly societies that appeared in Christchurch in the 1870s and 1880s.

One new religious sect gave Christchurch more than a little excitement in the 1890s, and enhanced its reputation as New Zealand's mecca for cranks and lost causes. Arthur Bently Worthington (his real name was Oakley Crawford) was an American bigamist and fraudster who arrived in Christchurch in 1890. He and his 'wife' Mary Plunkett founded a new church, the 'Students of Truth', and attracted a huge following with their persuasive preaching and theories of free love. Christchurch clergy made enquiries and uncovered Worthington's murky past (all of which he denied), and finally forced him to flee to Australia. When he tried to stage a comeback in Christchurch in September 1897, an angry crowd threatened a riot. (This was the only occasion on which the Riot Act has ever been read in Christchurch.) Disgraced and often imprisoned, he died in the USA in 1917, described as one of the era's 'most dangerous imposters'.

Christchurch claims the first telephone exchange in New Zealand, opened by a group of businessmen in 1881, and the city's streets began to be festooned with an ever-increasing forest of poles and wires. Electric lights made their first

Worthington's 'Temple of Truth' in Latimer Square, c. 1896. (The house on the left was also paid for by the fraudster's adoring Christchurch followers.) Designed by W. A. P. Clarkson and built in 1892, the hall survived until 1966 as the Latimer dance hall. The empty site has remained a carpark ever since.

J. G. Lamb photograph, CM 6479

Art Gallery, Durham Street (1890). The Canterbury Society of Arts raised the money to build this gallery by public subscription, and added another wing (right) by 1897, when this photograph was taken. Although the building survives, its ornamentation was later removed as an earthquake risk.

Wheeler and Son photograph, CM 4828

appearance on the Lyttelton wharves in 1882, and Ballantyne's became the city's first store illuminated by electricity in 1891. The first importation of a motor-car to Christchurch was in November 1898, and two years later Nicholas Oates received the city's first traffic-offence notice, for frightening a horse with his new vehicle.

Although many photographs of this period show nearly empty streets (pho-tographers preferred Sundays for street scenes), Christchurch was a busy place during the week, especially in the prosperous years of the late 1890s. Nearly all of the traffic was horse-drawn — drays, carts, hansom cabs, gigs, carriages and the occasional landau of a rich family — or human-powered. Bicycles were ubiqui-tous and knew no road rules. The American writer Mark Twain visited Christ-church in 1895 and quipped that half the citizens rode cycles, and kept the other half busy dodging them.

Extension of the steam-tram network encouraged the growth of several outer suburbs, notably Spreydon and Beckenham, but the most spectacular effect was on the seaside suburbs. Sumner was declared a borough in 1891, ahead of Lin-wood and Woolston (both 1893), while New Brighton's population grew rapidly after the tramline reached the beach in 1887. The construction of an ocean pier in 1894 boosted weekend excursions. New Brighton became a borough in 1897, and its population reached a thousand in 1901. St Albans achieved borough status in 1881, but Papanui never did, remaining something of a village until orcharding began to increase settlement in the 1890s.

South of the central city, St Martins, Beckenham and Somerfield began to attract more housing in the 1890s, but large open fields persisted in these parts well into the new century. Once the tramline reached the foot of Cashmere Hill

Opposite top: Lyttelton on 10 July 1895, after the 'Great Snow', which killed thousands of sheep in the Canterbury high country. Sheets of ice formed across the inner harbour. The long building in left foreground is the Harbour Board's coolstore.
Lyttelton Historical Society, CM 2452

Opposite bottom: City Council works yard, corner of Oxford Terrace and Worcester Street, c. 1899, before construction of the new Clarendon Hotel (to replace the wooden hotel under the trees at left). This yard also became a tram terminus before it was cleared and beautified for the Scott statue in 1917.
Brittenden collection, CHAC/CM 1217

Below: Captain Lorraine's balloon at Lancaster Park, 20 November 1899. This unfortunate aerial pioneer (whose real name was Mahoney) was blown out to sea and drowned off Godley Head. In the background is the famous No. 1 Stand (1882), which witnessed a host of Christchurch sporting events until its demolition in 1958.
CM 1303

Arthur Edgar Gravenor Rhodes (1859–1922), son of George Rhodes, pioneer of Banks Peninsula and South Canterbury. A leading Christchurch lawyer and philanthropist, he was Mayor of Christchurch in 1901 for the visit of the Duke and Duchess of York. Rhodes was a leading figure in the Order of St John, and established the first branch of the Red Cross in New Zealand, in Christchurch in 1915.

Hutton collection, CHAC/CM

Opposite top: High Street in the late 1890s, looking towards Morten's Building (1884–85), which later became the United Service Hotel. Note the muddy unsealed road and the abundance of telephone wires. The tramway was not electrified until 1903.

CM 12329

Bottom: New Zealand's Third Contingent for the Boer War trained in Christchurch at the Addington Showgrounds. Seen here in February 1900 marching to the Railway Station past Mrs Smith's Temperance Hotel and Johnston's Railway Hotel in Manchester Street.

F. W. Dutch photograph, Hean collection, CHAC/CM 433

in 1898, this became Christchurch's first hillside suburb, with a scattering of large houses dotting the slopes by 1903. It soon became a fashionable address for professionals and retired businessmen.

The closing years of the nineteenth century and the start of the twentieth were without doubt the halcyon years of Christchurch's identity as an outpost of the British Empire. Queen Victoria's Diamond Jubilee (1897) gave the city its biggest public celebrations to date, with military parades, concerts and dinners. A small military contingent sailed to England on the *Ruahine* to join the processions in London. To mark the jubilee, a clock tower was erected at the intersection of High and Manchester Streets. Intended for the Provincial Council Buildings, the clock had arrived from England in 1860 in 147 packages. It lay in storage for many years, and was given to the city council in 1876, which then could not agree on what to do with it, until 1897. (This was not the last resting place for the clock, however. In 1929 it was moved to its present location, the intersection of Victoria and Salisbury Streets.)

Patriotic sentiment reached new heights in 1899 with the outbreak of the Anglo–Boer War in South Africa. Canterbury's Volunteer movement was one of the strongest in New Zealand, and the Boer War was its first opportunity to take part in a real war overseas. Britain requested mounted troops from Australia and New Zealand, and Canterbury's prosperous elite soon provided ample funds for horses and equipment to enable volunteers to go to South Africa. The first contingent of 'Rough Riders' left Lyttelton in October 1899, to be followed by several more over the next two years. New Zealand's Third Contingent, of February 1900, was largely made up of Canterbury men.

The province celebrated its first jubilee in 1900. An exhibition was held in the newly built Canterbury Hall in Manchester Street in November, and civic celebrations held on 17 December gave rise to much self-congratulation. Even to the objective outsider's eye, there was indeed a great deal to feel pleased about. Survivors of the First Four Ships were now few and elderly, but they gladly reminded anyone who would listen that they had seen Cathedral Square when it was just open tussock, and Ferry Road when it was a muddy bullock track. The jubilee was promoted as a 'grand event', with processions and speeches and street decorations, and also stimulated the first serious attempt to collect and preserve the earliest records of the Canterbury settlement.

The death of Queen Victoria in January 1901 intensified the prevailing mood of Imperial loyalty, and added poignancy to the visit of the Duke and Duchess of Cornwall and York (later King George V and Queen Mary) in June. The Duke laid the foundation stone for a statue of Queen Victoria and reviewed a huge military parade in Hagley Park in pouring rain. Contingents representing all the regiments of the British Army visited Christchurch in February 1901 in the course of an Empire tour, and in March a group of turbaned Indian officers played in a polo match in Hagley Park, watched by a huge crowd. More crowds flocked to Lyttelton in November 1901 to meet the *Discovery* and Captain Robert Falcon Scott's first British Antarctic Expedition. This was the start of Christchurch's long involvement with Antarctic exploration, as the preferred city of departure for 'the Ice'. Yet more crowds waved Union Jacks in June 1902, to celebrate the end of the war in South Africa, and probably many of the same flags did duty again in August to celebrate the coronation of King Edward VII.

60

Right: Canterbury Hall (1900) on Manchester Street was a major civic project to mark the province's jubilee that year. This shows the admission booths for the Jubilee Exhibition. The building was gutted by fire in 1917, and new municipal offices were built behind the façade in the 1920s, and the Civic Theatre added later. The city council offices remained here until 1980.

Greenwood collection, CHAC/CM 495

Below: Jubilee Procession, 16 December 1900, at the corner of Armagh and Colombo Streets. S. Hurst Seager designed the decorations. Bullocks are hauling an old dray carrying descendants of the pre-Adamite settlers, proudly proclaiming, 'We were here first,' a reminder that the pre-eminence claimed by First Four Ships families did not go unchallenged.

Brittenden collection, CHAC/CM 1164

Imperial troops parade along Moorhouse Avenue, outside the Railway Station, in February 1901. Gasworks chimneys and gasometer are just visible in the distance at left.

CM 12567

In the last census before amalgamation in 1903, Christchurch City recorded 17,538 inhabitants, with another 28,288 in the boroughs of Sydenham, St Albans, Linwood, Woolston and New Brighton. Those parts of adjacent road boards which came within the Christchurch Health District added another 11,215, so that the whole metropolitan area of Christchurch and its suburbs boasted a population of 57,041. (By contrast, Lyttelton had 4,023 and Sumner just 844 residents). Christchurch was thus New Zealand's second-largest city: Auckland had 67,226 citizens, Dunedin 52,390 and Wellington 49,744. But the northern cities were growing faster. Since 1891 Christchurch had increased by 19 per cent, but Wellington had surged by 44 per cent.

'Hopeful' of 1887 (see page 52) might have formed some different conclusions about Christchurch in 1902. The central city was now almost fully built up and there were no 'slums', as that term was understood in London or New York, lined parks and avenues, and the beauty of the Avon winding through the central city. Christchurch had a better drainage system than any other New Zealand city, and typhoid was now virtually a disease of the past. The city was about to welcome electric trams and an abundant supply of electricity to match its abundant artesian water. The flat site meant that there were no natural obstacles to growth, as there were in Wellington: new industries could be set up in the suburbs, close to their labour force. It was claimed that workers in Christchurch were better fed and housed than in any other New Zealand city. A high proportion of its citizens owned their own homes, or were paying off mortgages rather than paying rent: a clear indication of New Zealand's trend towards a 'propertied democracy'. Edwardian Christchurch was an elegant colonial city, much improved from the dusty, disease-ridden frontier town of the 1870s.

63

CHAPTER FOUR

Progressive Christchurch

1903 – 1918

Henry Francis Wigram (1857–1934), grandson of a baronet, came to New Zealand in 1885. He was a successful businessman in Christchurch, owning the malt works at Heathcote and the *Lyttelton Times*. He was mayor in 1902–03, and supervised the amalgamation of nearby boroughs to form 'Greater Christchurch', but is now chiefly remembered as the father of the Royal New Zealand Air Force, for his pioneering support for aviation in the First World War and his gift of Sockburn Aerodrome, which became the Wigram Air Force Base.

Christchurch City Council

Opposite top: Edwardian Christchurch: Intersection of Lichfield (foreground), High and Manchester Streets, c. 1910. The Clock Tower was erected here in 1897 for Queen Victoria's Diamond Jubilee, and moved to its present site in Victoria Street in 1929.

F. W. Dutch photograph, F. W. Harris collection, CHAC/CM 172

Bottom: Laying tracks for the new electric trams in Cathedral Square, 1903. Under construction in the background is the Royal Exchange building, later known as the Regent Theatre building. Designed by the Luttrell brothers, it had the first electric elevator in Christchurch.

Canterbury Times photograph, CM 15561

Christchurch at last became a city in reality as well as in name in 1903, when the amalgamation of adjacent boroughs created 'Greater Christchurch'. This had been the particular campaign of Henry Wigram, who became first mayor of the enlarged city. From a strong manufacturing base, the city's economy and population grew steadily (eighty thousand by 1911), and its prosperity was demonstrated by a flourish of handsome new public and commercial buildings. Roads and drains were constantly improved, and in 1909 the city at last gained a high-pressure water supply. This era saw the advent of motorcars, electric trams and electric street lights. Yet it was also an era of civic beautification and growing concern for the environment, as seen in Harry Ell's Summit Road project, the preservation of Deans Bush and continued municipal tree-planting.

More is known in detail about Christchurch people, industries, businesses, clubs and institutions at the start of this period than at any other time before or since, thanks to the enterprise of a local publisher, Horace J. Weeks. The thousand-page Canterbury volume of his *Cyclopedia of New Zealand* (1903) is a treasure-trove of information about the city and its leading citizens, past and present, and provides an invaluable snapshot of Christchurch's industries and institutions in the early 1900s.

Edwardian Canterbury enjoyed prosperous times. The value of wool exported annually through Lyttelton doubled to £1.5 million, and that of frozen meat nearly doubled (even though the quantity increased by less than a quarter) because of rising prices. As the province prospered, so too did Christchurch. Farmers could afford to buy new machinery, thus boosting the city's engineering sector, while their wives spent more at the big department stores like Ballantyne's, Beath's and the DIC, enabling all three to erect new buildings in 1908–09. Apart from the 1907 freezing works dispute and a short sharp slump in 1909, employment remained buoyant. As railway projects ended on the Midland and Waipara–Cheviot lines, there was plenty of work available in Christchurch on drainage and other civic works, and on building sites: inner Christchurch had a building boom in the early 1900s.

The city's most prominent landmark, the Anglican Cathedral, was at last being completed with the addition of apse and transepts when the Cheviot earthquake of 16 November 1901 damaged the spire (yet again). Rather than simply replace the stonework, it was decided to rebuild the upper section in timber sheathed in copper, to reduce the risk of future earthquake damage.

Once again the Rhodes family paid for the repairs. The completed Cathedral was opened with great ceremony and rejoicing on 1 November 1904. In the meantime, Christchurch's Roman Catholic Pro-Cathedral had been hauled to one side by traction engines to make room for an impressive new basilica in Oamaru stone, designed by F. W. Petre. Opened in February 1905, this is widely regarded as New Zealand's finest Renaissance-style building. When George Bernard Shaw visited the city in 1934, he complimented his hosts on their splendid cathedral. They assumed he meant the one in Cathedral Square. 'No,' he replied, 'the one down by the gasworks.'

Cathedral of the Blessed Sacrament, Barbadoes Street, under construction in 1902. Designed by F. W. Petre in 1899 and completed in 1905, this is one of New Zealand's finest churches and its most important example of French-Italian Renaissance architecture.

CM 4603

66

Another city landmark of this period is the statue of Queen Victoria, unveiled in May 1903. Market Square was renamed Victoria Square in her memory. All around, the streets were being dug up to lay lines for the new electric trams. In 1905, to replace the old drill shed, the Defence Department built the King Edward Barracks on Cashel Street, near the police station. This gave Christchurch its largest public covered floor space for many years to come, a venue for anything from flower shows to choral concerts. The roof was supported by curved steel lattice-work ribs, and was raised in less than a month. The tallest of the commercial buildings which sprouted in the inner city at this time was the New

Unveiling Queen Victoria's statue, 25 May 1903. Market Square was now renamed Victoria Square. Rink Stables' Armagh Street entrance is prominent, next to Treleaven's hay and grain store, a major supplier to the city's working horses, all soon to disappear. The Cathedral spire is still under repair after the 1901 Cheviot earthquake.

Wigram Collection, Macmillan Brown Library, University of Canterbury

67

Zealand Express Company building in Hereford Street (1906), designed by the Luttrell brothers. Although modest by American standards, it was promptly dubbed Christchurch's 'skyscraper', and remained a prominent feature on the city's skyline for several decades. Also in 1906, H. Hampton's statue of William Rolleston was unveiled on a key site in front of the Museum, at the end of Worcester Street, and the avenue was named after him. (His grim expression is probably because hardly anyone now pronounces his surname correctly.)

R. J. ('King Dick') Seddon, New Zealand's portly premier, had decided as early as 1903 that the country should advertise itself to promote trade and tourism by means of a lavishly funded international exhibition. Christchurch was chosen as the ideal venue, and Seddon gave the project top priority. The city responded by setting up a range of committees to plan the exhibition down to the last detail, with unlimited advice and money from the government. The result was highly successful, an event of great importance for New Zealand's emerging sense of national identity. For Christchurch it was quite simply the greatest show the city had ever seen, bringing a welcome influx of visitors and their money.

It was decided that the buildings would all be temporary and the site completely cleared once the exhibition was over. The leading Christchurch architect Joseph Clarkson Maddison won the commission and produced a spectacular French Renaissance-style design covering nearly fourteen acres, with towers and domes facing the River Avon and Park Terrace. The exterior was clad in gleaming white 'Stuccoline' panels, made from a mixture of plaster, hemp and cement, giving an impression of permanence. Tonnes of plaster were used to make elaborate entablatures and pilasters, and thousands of cubic meters of pre-cut timber were used in the framework of the buildings, delivered by a temporary railway line laid across Hagley Park. One of the entrance towers had an electric elevator to give visitors views of the city. The whole complex was at the time the largest structure ever built in New Zealand. The galleries were filled with the products of the British Empire as well as New Zealand; the Canadian and Australian contributions were especially notable. Several government departments had their own displays, with the prevailing theme of 'Progress'. The Railway Department's display included a new steam locomotive made at the Addington Railway Workshops.

Several new hotels were built in anticipation of the expected influx of visitors for the Exhibition. Two 1880s hotels opposite the Bank of New Zealand on Morten's Corner were bought by a Boer War veteran, Lieutenant-Colonel Jowsey, and combined into one large hotel, which he named the United Service Hotel. This luxurious establishment boasted an electric elevator and remained a landmark in the Square for the next eighty years, rivalling the Clarendon Hotel (1901) as the city's most prestigious accommodation. Britain's Exhibition Commissioner Sir John Gorst was fulsome in his praise of Christchurch's support for the event. Many visitors viewing the city from one of the Exhibition towers remarked on all the trees they could see, and Christchurch was commonly known as the 'City of Trees' at this time. But Gorst spoke of a 'Garden City', and the name has stuck ever since.

Music flourished in Edwardian Christchurch. The Exhibition gave a great boost to orchestral music-making, and in 1908 Benno Scherek helped form

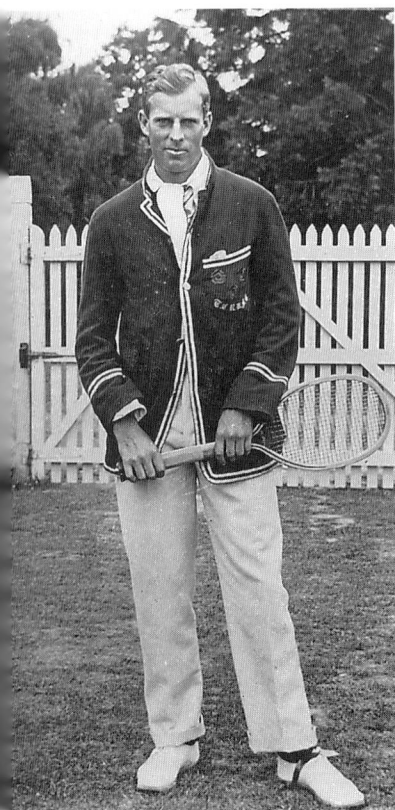

Frederick Anthony Wilding (1883–1915) was New Zealand's most successful tennis player. Born in Christchurch, he gained a Cambridge law degree but went into commerce. He won the men's singles at Wimbledon 1910–13, and was in the Davis Cup winning team in 1907, 1909 and 1914. He was a captain in the Intelligence Corps when killed at Ypres.

Christchurch Star

Above: The New Zealand International Exhibition, Christchurch, 1906–07. Main building, designed by J. C. Maddison. The central towers were illuminated at night by hundreds of electric lights. All of these buildings were demolished and the site remains empty, part of North Hagley Park.

Christchurch Star

Below: View west along Kilmore Street looking across the Victoria Street intersection towards the entrance to the Exhibition. Spires of the Normal School on the right. This part of the city did not quite match the gleaming white splendour of the Exhibition towers. The site on the left is now occupied by the Parkroyal Hotel.

C. Beken photograph, CM 3902

View south-east from the Cathedral tower, c. 1910, showing at left the New Zealand Express Company building (1906) on the corner of Manchester and Hereford Streets. This was Christchurch's first 'skyscraper'. Cathedral of the Blessed Sacrament beyond in the distance, its copper domes still darkly new.

Brittenden collection, CHAC/CM 1199

the Christchurch Orchestral Society. But concerts, opera and traditional theatre now faced a new competitor, which was destined to dominate the twentieth century: the movies. Edison's 'kinematograph' was first demonstrated in Christchurch in 1896, and as early as 1901 the visit of the Duke and Duchess of Cornwall and York was recorded on moving film in Christchurch. The Colosseum in Armagh Street, a former skating rink which had been O'Brien's boot factory and then a cab rank, became Christchurch's first picture theatre in May 1908. As silent movies caught the public imagination and grew rapidly in popularity, Christchurch acquired a variety of new theatres, starting with Queen's in 1912. The Grand (later the Embassy) was built in the Square the following year, as were Everybody's (later renamed the Tivoli) in 1915 and the Strand (later the Plaza) in 1917. The interiors of these theatres were often sumptuous when they first opened, but there was an ever-present risk of fire from primitive projectors and inflammable early film. Going to the movies in Edwardian Christchurch was not without an element of risk; but so was riding on a tram, because of the long pins women used to secure the large hats of that period.

Christchurch's worst inner-city fire to that date occurred in February 1908. It started in Strange's department store at night, and the fire brigade could not prevent it from spreading to adjacent buildings. By dawn the blaze had consumed most of a major city block, destroying Ashby Bergh's, the DIC and the White Hart Hotel. Insurance companies paid out over £300,000, making this New Zealand's most expensive fire to that date. Hoses had been laid along Cashel Street to draw water from the Avon, but the brigade's pumps could not cope. This disastrous fire hastened the city's high-pressure water system (completed in June 1909), but it was not the first serious fire of this period. In

70

Aftermath of Strange's fire, February 1908, showing the burnt-out shell of the DIC and scorched wall of Beath's. This was Christchurch's biggest fire to date, and destroyed half of an inner-city block. The city's high-pressure water supply was completed in 1909.

Brittenden collection, CHAC/CM 1209

December 1905 most of the Woolston tanneries were destroyed by fire, despite being right beside the Heathcote River, and in November 1907 the Kaiapoi Woollen Mills factory in Cashel Street burned down. In January 1908 the Hyman Marks building at Christchurch Hospital was seriously damaged in a blaze, making people wonder if there was an arsonist at large.

By 1900 the City Council had at long last realised that it could not indefinitely carry on with a sealed-pan system of sewage disposal. The drainage board submitted a plan to extend the underground sewers, but the other local bodies, as usual, were unwilling to contribute funds. The city went ahead, however, and raised a loan of £25,000 to let the first sewer contract since 1884, and four more contracts followed. The inner-city network was completed by 1903, when 3,622 houses were connected to 48 miles of sewers. After another delay, while

No shortage of water here! Waltham Road, 30 March 1909, looking north towards the Cathedral of the Blessed Sacrament. Railway goods sheds on the left, gasworks chimneys on the right. This area was prone to flooding until the completion of a major stormwater relief scheme in the late 1960s.

F. W. Hulme photograph, Bougen collection, CHAC/CM 117

Bonnington's the Chemists was a household name, not only in Christchurch but throughout Australasia, thanks to their 'Irish Moss Cough Mixture', manufactured in a modest factory (still there) in Olliviers Road, near Ferry Road. This is the interior of their city shop, c. 1910.

Bonningtons collection, CM 15395

Aulsebrook's was another household name by 1913, when this photograph was taken of its enlarged factory on the corner of St Asaph and Montreal Streets. As the crowd of staff suggests, this firm was one of the city's major employers.

Aulsebrook album,. CM 13923

the tramway was being built, another flurry of sewer construction from 1906 covered a wide area of the suburbs, so that by the end of 1914 there were 12,844 houses connected to over a hundred miles of sewers. Half the connections had been made since 1909, thanks to the new water supply available from June that year. Christchurch was a much healthier city as a result.

Electricity had ceased to be a novelty but could still amaze by its sheer spectacle: the Exhibition buildings had been floodlit at night, and the Cathedral spire was strung with coloured lights for special occasions. The extension

of cheap household electricity came on the eve of the First World War, after the completion of the government's first major hydro-power station at Lake Coleridge in 1914. The first regular supply reached the city in April 1915, and the city's first electric street lights were switched on a month later.

Christchurch's most prominent politicians of this era were Harry Ell and Tommy Taylor. Both appealed to working-class voters, and both were outspoken critics of conservatism and caution. As Postmaster-General, Ell gave Christchurch its first coin-operated public telephones in 1911, only a few years after its first coin-operated stamp vending machines. But he is best remembered now for the Summit Road around the Port Hills. Ell lobbied tirelessly (some might say obsessively) for his vision of a road around the tops from Godley Head to Akaroa, persuading landowners to donate land and to preserve the few remaining patches of native bush.

Tommy Taylor (also known as 'Tea' Taylor, from his initials and his temperance campaigns) was already Christchurch's leading radical politician and social reformer. He was one of the country's most effective speakers: as one reporter put it, 'Just as the average politician is naturally dull, Taylor is naturally vivid and exciting.' His decision to stand for the Christchurch mayoralty in 1911 caused a stir. Charles Allison had tried hard to be a progressive mayor (1908–10) but often supported lost causes. Taylor won easily and threw himself wholeheartedly into the job, pushing for housing reform and tarsealed roads, but within three months he died suddenly after an operation. The whole city was stunned to lose such a popular mayor, and Taylor's funeral cortège was the longest the city had ever seen. As Canterbury's centennial history states: 'No citizen has made a deeper impact on both civic and national affairs.'

Another death that stunned the city and gave Christchurch one of its most-photographed public monuments was that of the Antarctic explorer Captain Robert Falcon Scott. Lyttelton had become the favoured setting-off point for British Antarctic exploration, but Scott's 1910–12 expedition, which left Lyttelton on the *Terra Nova*, ended in disappointment and tragedy. Amundsen beat him to the South Pole, and on his return journey Scott and his companions perished in the snow. The first news of his death reached Christchurch in February 1913, and plunged the city into deep mourning. Scott's diary revealed how courageously he and his companions had faced certain death, making them heroes throughout the British Empire. His widow sculpted a memorial statue in England which was later copied for Christchurch; it was unveiled on Oxford Terrace in February 1917.

The Antarctic expeditions often drew crowds to Lyttelton, and thousands of Christchurch people had their first good look at a battleship in February 1913, when HMS *New Zealand* spent a week at Lyttelton. This was the dreadnought which Sir Joseph Ward's government had gifted to the Royal Navy. The visit created as much interest and patriotic fervour as a royal tour. Virtually every school in Canterbury sent pupils to tour the battle cruiser, thanks to free rail passes, and at night the warship's powerful searchlights lit up the Port Hills. Lyttelton was again the focus of attention in October and November 1913 when a lock-out on the Wellington wharves spread to other ports. In Christchurch there was a massive mobilisation of volunteers and farmers to keep the port open. The Addington Showgrounds became a camp for the 'Specials' and their

Henry George Ell (1862–1934), soldier, printer, stationer, politician and conservationist, was the tireless promoter of the Summit Road along the Port Hills, as well as many other social and environmental reforms.
CM E67

Thomas Edward Taylor (1862–1911) came to New Zealand in 1873 and trained for the Methodist ministry, but was regarded as 'too unorthodox and argumentative'. He then became one of the country's leading prohibitionists (with Leonard Isitt) and entered Parliament in 1896. Tommy Taylor was one of the best public speakers of his day, deeply committed to social reform. Elected Mayor of Christchurch in 1911, he died unexpectedly after three months' frenetic activity.
CHAC/CM 941

Oxford Terrace, near Cashel Street, 1913. Special constables (mostly farmers and Territorials) make a show of strength during the waterfront strike. They camped at the Addington Showgrounds and kept the wharves working at Lyttelton with little of the violence seen in Wellington or Auckland. Many of these men a year later rode back to Lyttelton in uniform to leave for the First World War with the First NZ Expeditionary Force.

CM 7640

Opposite top: Little is known about Louis W. Bloy or the fate of his Christchurch Ladies' Banjo Band, but it is only one example of numerous musical groups active in Edwardian Christchurch. Mrs Rose Bloy is the third lady from the left.

Hough collection, CHAC/CM 30

Bottom: Nurse Sibylla Maude (fourth from right) established New Zealand's first district nursing scheme in 1896 and became one of Christchurch's best-known and most-admired women. Here she is in 1914 with seven of her nurses outside their headquarters in Durham Street South. In 1919 they moved into a new building in Madras Street funded by the Rhodes family.

CM 4588

horses. After several noisy confrontations between strikers and Specials, a force of seven hundred occupied the wharves on 25 November to move essential supplies and exports. (Aulsebrook's biscuit factory had closed because of the sugar shortage.) Apart from minor scuffles, Christchurch did not have the level of violence seen in Wellington, probably because the city was at a distance from its port, but the political polarisation between workers and 'capitalists' left a long and bitter legacy.

As part of the British Empire, New Zealand found itself at war with Germany on 4 August 1914. Everyone expected it to be a short and victorious war. Since conscription had been introduced in 1909, New Zealand's territorial forces had been training for just such an event, and hundreds of young men rushed to volunteer for overseas service. Large patriotic processions boosted the mood of jingoistic war fever during August, and the first Canterbury troops for the First New Zealand Expeditionary Force sailed from Lyttelton on 23 September. They expected to go to Europe but were diverted to defend the Suez Canal against the Turks, and it was here, in February 1915, that the Canterbury Battalion sustained New Zealand's first casualties of the Great War. From Egypt the troops were sent with the Australians to seize the Dardanelles, and landed at Gallipoli on 25 April 1915. The resulting bloodbath is still commemorated every Anzac Day. Many more New Zealanders were to be killed on the Western Front in France and Belgium from 1916 to 1918.

Canterbury's military contribution to the Great War amounted to nearly 24,000 men enlisted. The Canterbury Regiment lost 386 men killed (including its commander, Lieutenant-Colonel D. McBean Stewart) at Gallipoli, and two more battalions which served in France lost 58 officers and 1,386 other ranks killed in action. Another 575 died from wounds and disease. The Canterbury Mounted Rifles served with distinction in Palestine, where 334 men died. Altogether Canterbury lost 2,739 men in the Great War.

74

CHRISTCHURCH LADIES' BANJO BAND, 1913.
LOUIS W. BLOY, Conductor.

DISTRICT NURSING OFFICE.
HOURS 9 TO 10AM 2 TO 3 P.M.
Messages may be left any time.

Moncks Bay, Redcliffs, with Shag Rock at left, c. 1910.

Barr collection, CM 583

Sydenham, 'the model borough', c. 1914, showing the tower for its water supply, and Sydenham Park,
Christchurch's first A&P Showgrounds. Housing spread rapidly on Cashmere Hill after 1900.

Alexander Turnbull Library, Wellington, G5377

Men of the Eighth Reinforcement, NZEF, parade through Cathedral Square on 21 November 1915. United Service Hotel in the background.

Weekly Press, CM 151089

Papanui Buildings, 1913. This was one of the grander suburban shopping developments that followed tramline extensions in Christchurch (Westminster Street in St Albans has another).

Read collection, CHAC/CM 893

Meat and meat products have always been major Canterbury exports, giving employment to hundreds of Christchurch workers. Here a diminutive Barclay locomotive pulls three meat wagons from the Islington freezing works, c. 1914.

Wright collection, CHAC/CM 234

78

The war also gave Christchurch its first aerodrome. Henry Wigram had become fascinated by aeroplanes when on a visit to England in 1908, but failed to persuade the New Zealand government to set up a flying school. The war convinced him that aviation had an important future and, as the government would still not help, he went ahead with a private venture. A suitable field was bought at Sockburn, three Caudron biplanes were ordered from England in 1916, and an instructor was hired from Hendon. The first intake of students arrived in June 1917, and by the end of the war 182 pilots had been trained at Sockburn, nearly all of whom joined the Royal Flying Corps. Wigram was determined to see the aviation school continue in peacetime.

Christchurch's home-front war effort from 1915 until the end of the war was unprecedented and highly successful. Businessmen and community leaders who had helped make the 1906–07 Exhibition such a triumph now turned their organisational skills to fund-raising for the war, and the women of Christchurch responded likewise, rolling bandages, knitting socks and balaclavas, and packing parcels of 'trench comforts' for the men overseas. The St John Ambulance Association took an early lead in this work, and in May 1915 Arthur Rhodes established the first New Zealand branch of the Red Cross Society in Christchurch. They launched a new appeal and raised £7,500 within two months, to send to the Red Cross parent body in London. In February 1916 the Red Cross and St John joined forces for the duration of the war, and raised over £200,000. The YMCA was another major fund-raiser, and a queen carnival held over several months in 1916 raised £135,000. The savings from Canterbury's prosperous years were largely swallowed up by the Great War.

The war years also tested the loyalty of left-wing political groups. Christchurch had been an important centre for the growth of trade unions and the Labour Party in New Zealand. Dan Sullivan's Labour Political League of 1908 had renamed itself the New Zealand Labour Party, only to become the United

Ettie Rout (1877–1936). Born in Tasmania, she was well known in Christchurch in the early 1900s as an accomplished shorthand typist. First editor of *The Maoriland Worker* (1910), she, ironically, became notorious rather than famous for campaigning to reduce venereal disease among New Zealand troops in France during the First World War. She married Christchurch physiotherapist Fred Hornibrook in 1920.

CM 7530

Aviation in Christchurch really began on 23 December 1911 when George Bolt flew two large hang-gliders from Cashmere Hill. In March 1914 J. W. H. Scotland flew a Caudron biplane to Christchurch from Timaru. Here it is, with another pioneer aviator, James Edward Moore, at the Sockburn Aerodrome in 1914.

J. T. Mitchell photograph, Taylor collection, CHAC/CM 360

Right: Red Cross fund-raising in Cathedral Square, 1917. Christchurch and Canterbury raised huge amounts of money to assist New Zealand soldiers serving overseas during the First World War.

Alexander Turnbull Library, Wellington, 17664-1/1

Below: Patriotic pupils at Elmwood School, 1918. Note the small US flag pinned to the New Zealand flag. While battleships are all the rage in the front row, the child at right in the back row has made an unusual flying machine.

CM 9520

Labour Party in 1912, representing the moderates of the trades councils. The militant wing of the labour movement, the so-called 'Red Feds', discredited by the defeats of Waihi and the waterfront dispute of 1913, had formed the Socialist Democratic Party, and one of its leaders, James McCombs (MP for Lyttelton, 1913–33), became a powerful influence in the combined Labour Party of 1916. Some of their supporters held radical socialist and pacifist views, but risked official wrath if they stated them too openly. Resistance to conscription of married men gained strong public support towards the end of the war, with large public meetings and a near-riot at the King Edward Barracks in April 1918, when a crowd of women tried to prevent the departure of the first draft of married men to serve overseas.

The last years of the Great War saw the further growth of 'Greater Christchurch'. Opawa joined the city in October 1916, followed by Avonside and St Martins in 1917. Deans Bush was officially opened as a public reserve on 24

The first aerial photograph of Christchurch, taken by Leslie Hinge from 2,400 feet on 17 January 1918. Latimer Square at left, and the smoking Destructor chimney centre foreground. King Edward Barracks (1905) and Canterbury College are prominent in the middle distance.
CM

Ada Wells (1863–1933), teacher and journalist, was the first woman to become a Christchurch city councillor, the second to join the Charitable Aid Board, and one of the first on the Hospital Board. She was secretary to the National Council of Women and helped found the Children's Aid Society.

Steffano Webb photograph, CM 10509

George Warren Russell (1854–1937), journalist, newspaper proprietor and politician. Known as 'Riccarton' (later 'Rickety') Russell, he was MP for Riccarton 1893–96, 1899–1902, and Avon 1908–19. As Minister of Public Health 1915–19 he bore the brunt of public criticism over the 1918 influenza epidemic.

CM

February 1917. Mrs Ada Wells became the first woman city councillor that year, and in March 1918 the Canterbury Progress League held its first meeting, to consider the postwar development of the city. The Godley statue was moved across the Square to a new site beside the Cathedral, to make way for a redevelopment project that was then abandoned after public protest. Two heavy snowfalls in July cut the Lake Coleridge electricity supply and gave Christchurch its coldest day on record (22 July). By late October the end of the war was in sight.

But Christchurch was then faced with a different sort of crisis, which completely overshadowed the Armistice. A new strain of mild influenza had swept around the world in the middle of 1918. Somehow the virus became much more deadly in the Northern Hemisphere autumn – perhaps by exposure to mustard gas on the Western Front – and a very destructive second wave swept the entire globe in the last months of 1918. It was called 'Spanish influenza', not because it started there, but because the King of Spain was an early survivor. Millions of others were not so fortunate. This was the world's worst-ever pandemic of influenza, killing an estimated 25 million people, mostly young adults. The second wave reached New Zealand in October, probably on returning troopships, and spread rapidly. Because influenza was not then a notifiable dangerous disease, there was no attempt to halt the ferries or to quarantine the South Island.

Unfortunately for Christchurch, early November coincided with Show Week, and hundreds of racegoers from the North Island came south for the races, bringing the infection with them. At least the city had some warning, from the sudden worsening of the epidemic in Auckland and Wellington, but apart from a useless atomised zinc sulphate spray, the health authorities had no answer to the killer flu. Friday 8 November was People's Day at the Show; it was also the day when a false report of the Armistice brought huge crowds into Cathedral Square to celebrate, only to wander home when the news was contradicted.

This was probably the point of maximum spread of the infection, and over that weekend half the city seemed to fall ill with the flu. Hotels crowded with visitors began to look like hospitals. Doctors and nurses were run off their feet. This flu struck suddenly, and some victims died within days, or even hours. Most of those who developed pneumonia were dead within a week. Yet, amazingly, when the official Armistice news arrived on 12 November, Christchurch went ahead with long-laid plans for a procession and rally in the Square. The Cathedral bells rang for victory, even as people were dying in hotels nearby.

For a fortnight after the Armistice, normal life was suspended in Christchurch. Many shops and factories closed as staff fell ill, or to release the able-bodied for relief work. Banks were shut by government decree for a week, and all hotels, billiard rooms and theatres were closed to prevent further spread of infection. The streets were often empty, except for the odd ambulance or relief car. Fourteen tramcars were stationed at suburban termini to serve as inhalation chambers. The worst day of the epidemic was 19 November, when forty-eight victims died. Thereafter the death toll declined as quickly as it had soared. Over five hundred people died in Christchurch during the terrible 'Spanish Influenza' of November 1918. Some of these were visitors, stranded during Show Week, or country people brought by ambulance to the hospital; a few Christchurch folk died in other towns. The final reckoning found 806 flu deaths in Canterbury; 458 of these were residents of Christchurch.

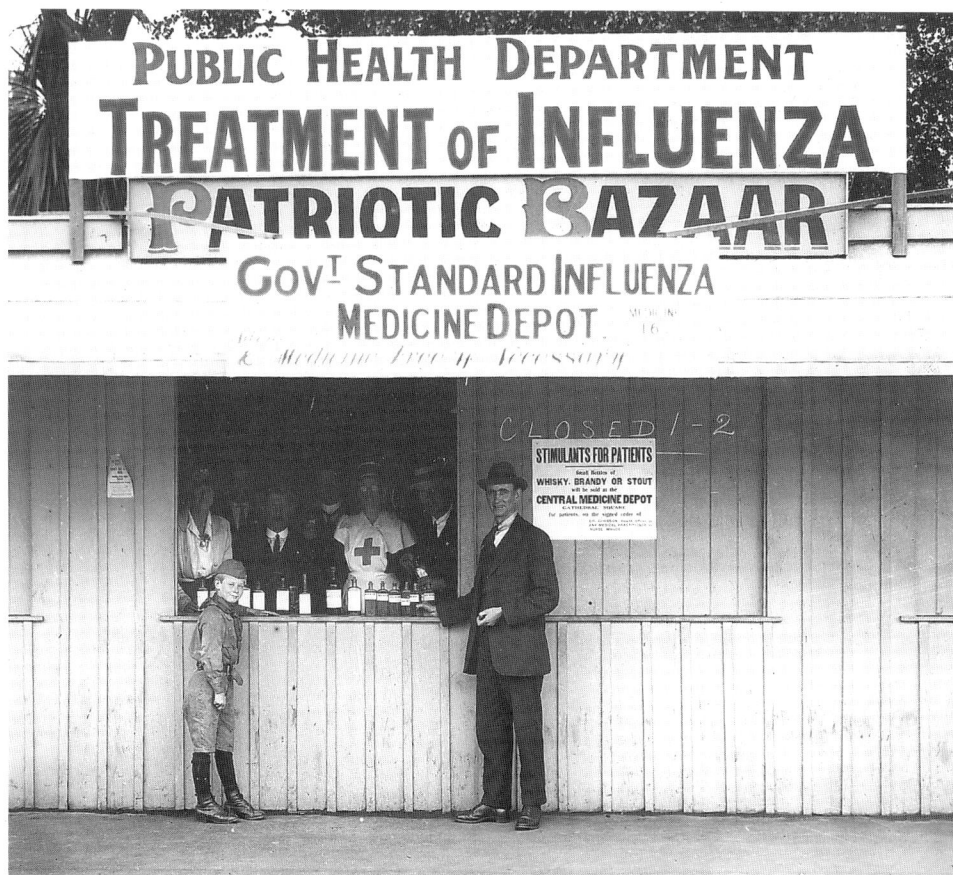

Left: The Patriotic Bazaar in Cathedral Square has become the 'Government Standard Influenza Medicine Depot'. This photograph was taken on 4 December 1918.

ATL, *Christchurch Press* collection, 8542-1/1

Below: Nurse Maude's Central Bureau, Cathedral Square. The Automobile Association provided cars and drivers to take exhausted doctors and nurses on their rounds. The streets were sprayed with disinfectant.

ATL, *Christchurch Press* collection, 8546-1/1

This was Christchurch's worst-ever public health crisis, and its worst natural disaster in terms of mortality. (By comparison, the 1931 Napier earthquake killed 256 people in Hawke's Bay province.) In the rest of the country, over two thousand Maori died in the 1918 flu, about four per cent of their total population at that time. European deaths totalled 6,091, while 322 New Zealand soldiers died of influenza while overseas.

The epidemic relief organisation gradually disbanded early in December 1918, as the city returned to normal, just in time for Christmas shopping. But it was a far-from-festive season in many Christchurch households, and life could not return to pre-war normality for those bereaved. The war and the influenza epidemic had left too many gaps and shattered too many lives. Most people just wanted to forget the last four years and get on with the future. Perhaps this is why Christchurch took so long to decide on a suitable war memorial, and finished up with two. But nobody thought of a memorial to the 458 citizens who had died in the 'Black Flu'. It was still too frightful and recent to need any reminders.

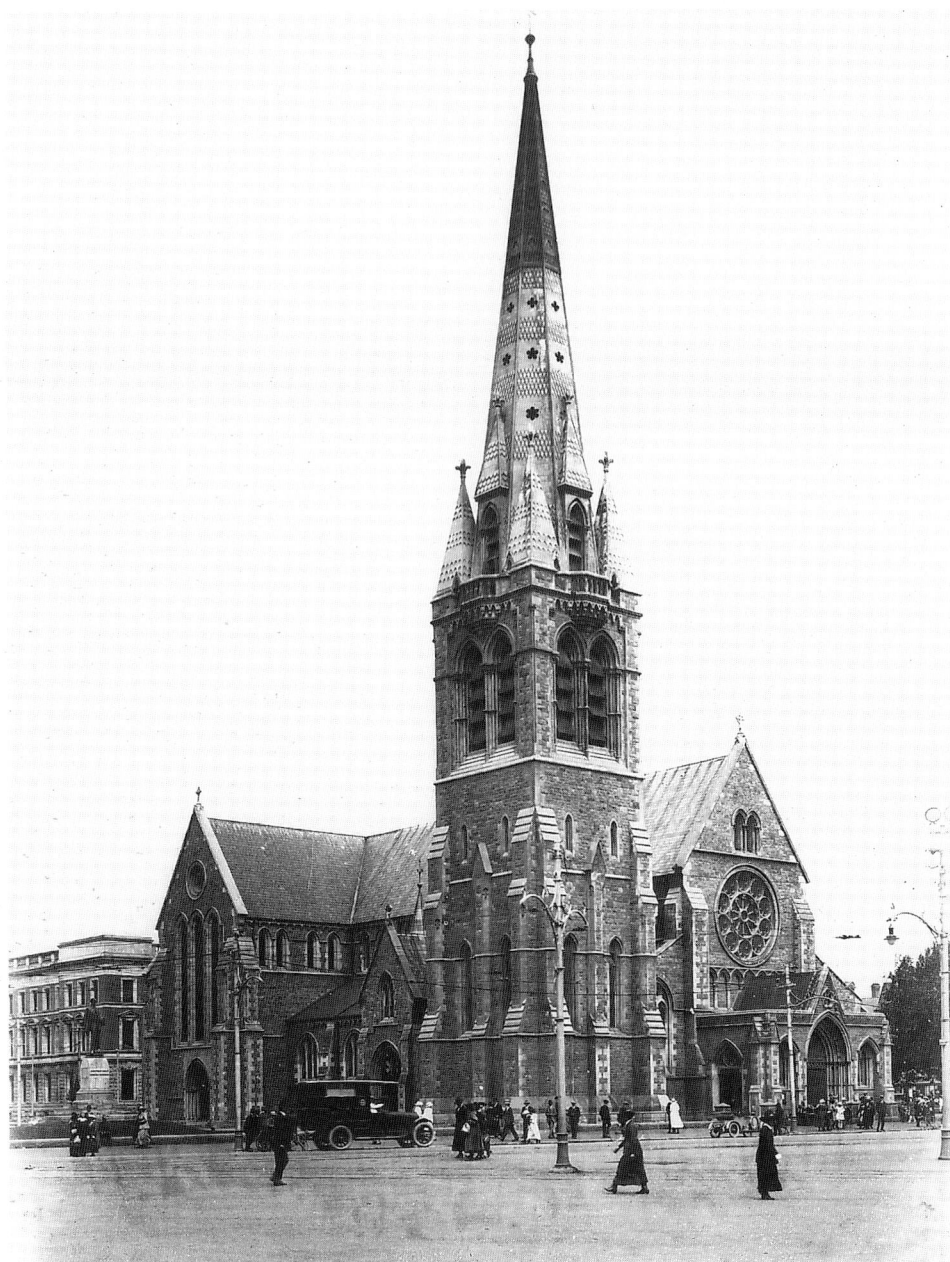

Christchurch Cathedral, November 1918; a St John ambulance is passing in front of the Cathedral. Note the position of the Godley statue, where the Citizens' War Memorial now stands.

W. A. Taylor photograph, CM

CHAPTER FIVE

Garden City

1919 – 1939

People born in Christchurch in the shadow of the Great War and the 1918 influenza epidemic grew up in disconcerting times. While old continuities persisted in much of daily life, this was a period of great changes and contrasts, which included Christchurch's worst-ever economic recession, mass unemployment and street violence. Christchurch was the first New Zealand city to have a Labour mayor and council before the 1935 general election ushered in the first Labour government and the welfare state. Several historians have claimed that Christchurch treated its unemployed better than any other city, and that the streets were peaceful compared with the riots in Auckland and Wellington. The reality was not so rosy: Christchurch's 1932 tramway strike was a far-from-peaceful protest, and unemployment disputes involved two deaths, while the

Thomas Edmonds' 'Sure to Rise' baking-powder factory, Ferry Road, 1920. One of Christchurch's most famous icons, the factory was renowned for its superb gardens, but the company moved to Auckland in 1983 and Brierley Investments demolished the building in 1990. A petrol station now occupies the site.
Thomson photograph, Adam collection, CHAC/CM 926

Henry Thomas Joynt Thacker (1870–1939) was born at Okains Bay and educated at Christchurch Boys' High School and Canterbury College before completing a medical degree at Edinburgh. He was a noted footballer and first president of the Canterbury Rugby Football League, and helped train Richard Arnst, who became the world's champion sculler in 1910. Thacker was MP for Christchurch East (1914–22) and one of Christchurch's most colourful mayors (1919–23), leading the Port Christchurch campaign.

CHAC/CM 977

Opposite top: Opening of the Bridge of Remembrance, 11 November 1924. King Edward Barracks upper right.

CM 14572

Bottom: Visit of HRH the Prince of Wales, seen here on 16 May 1920. This car was Frank McTeigue's taxi before he went off to war.

McTeigue collection, CHAC/CM 264

City Council preferred to amass reserves rather than spend more on relief works. It was a city of paradoxes: a Labour stronghold, yet deeply conservative; a progressive go-ahead place which always seemed to die on Sundays; a wealthy city full of poor people; a garden city with roads full of potholes.

This was also an age of exciting new technologies: of electricity and radio, of motor cars and aeroplanes, of aspirin and ice cream and things made from plastic. Huge crowds still gathered to watch rugby matches and election results, and to gawp at royal visitors, but radio enabled more people to be entertained at home. Weekends were usually divided between sport and gardening. Most houses stood on large sections, with a flower garden at the front and a lawn and vegetable garden in the back yard. Encouraged by the Horticultural Society and regular newspaper gardening columns, many householders made their front gardens bloom spectacularly in this period. But in the grim years of the Depression many families fed themselves largely on what they could grow in the back garden. Gardening for them was a serious necessity.

Christchurch led New Zealand in several fields of endeavour in this period. In aviation, it had the country's first air base and welcomed the first successful flight from Australia. In the cultural sphere, Christchurch was home to a significant renaissance in art, drama and literature. Despite the economic recession of the 1930s, this was a notable period of civic enhancement, when such landmarks as the Captain Cook statue, the Robert McDougall Art Gallery and the Edmonds Band Rotunda made their appearance. Although more people departed than arrived in the early thirties, over the period as a whole the city's population grew by a third, from just over 100,000 in 1919 to 135,000 in 1939.

The First World War did not officially end until the conclusion of the Versailles Peace Treaty in 1919, so Christchurch's civic celebrations to mark the end of the Great War did not take place until 19 July. Already the city was debating the nature of its permanent war memorial, and as usual on such matters the city divided itself into two stubborn and argumentative camps. Two rival fund-raising committees emerged: one wanted a cenotaph in the middle of Cathedral Square; the other wanted something useful, such as a bridge. Unable to decide between them, the city council recognised both schemes. The utilitarian memorial was first to become a reality and, apart from the Cathedral, is one of the city's most distinctive landmarks: the Bridge of Remembrance was opened in November 1924. The Cenotaph project suffered many delays, not least from the economic depression of the early 1930s, and was not unveiled until 1937.

In a move widely seen as King George V's personal thanks to the dominions for their immense sacrifices in the war, the Prince of Wales (later Edward VIII) was sent on a tour of the Empire in 1920. He came to Christchurch in May, to be welcomed by the new mayor, Dr Henry Thacker, one of the city's more colourful and outspoken leaders. The Prince had come to Christchurch by train from the West Coast, but as the Otira Tunnel was not yet finished, he had to traverse Arthur's Pass by stage coach. When completed in October 1921, the tunnel was the seventh longest in the world, and the longest outside Europe. The Midland Line was finally opened on 4 August 1923 and had an immediate effect on Christchurch. West Coast coal and timber could now reach the city directly, instead of by sea, and new coal yards sprang up along Moorhouse Avenue. Cheaper coal meant increased domestic and industrial use, adding to

Cathedral Square, 1921, looking east. Everybody's Cinema at left, Post Office right foreground. The New Zealand Express building is still the only tall building on the skyline.

R. Verey Scott photograph, Kim collection, CHAC/CM 703

the smoke created by the railways (and the council's rubbish destructor). Christchurch's winter smog worsened, and has remained a major environmental problem ever since.

The influenza epidemic left a legacy of increased public concern for fresh air and healthy living. In 1924 Fendalton School was the first in the country to add 'open-air' classrooms, to a standard design which allowed one wall to be folded back on warm sunny days (and not-so-warm ones, if your teacher was a fresh-air fanatic). Some people turned to faith healing and alternative medicines: enormous crowds attended the Hickson Mission in the grounds of the Cathedral in 1923, and many South Island Maori joined the Ratana Church, which had its origins in the epidemic. A polio outbreak that killed twenty-seven people and disabled many more in Canterbury in 1925 warned that influenza was not the only unpredictable disease around, but tuberculosis was still the most-feared scourge of the 1920s: the children's open-air ward at the Cashmere Sanatorium was opened in October 1923. In 1925 Christchurch held its first 'Health Week', an attempt to educate the public about nutrition and hygiene through lectures, demonstrations and newspaper articles. Christchurch cannot

claim to have started the Health Camp movement in New Zealand, but Cora Wilding's Sunlight League (1931) was an important precursor.

The royal tour of 1927 was rather a let-down for Christchurch. After their triumphal tour of the North Island, the Duke and Duchess of York (later George VI and Elizabeth, the Queen Mother) were eagerly awaited in Christchurch. But the Duchess fell ill in Nelson and had to return to Wellington. The Duke therefore laid the foundation stone of the Nurses' Memorial Chapel at Christchurch Hospital, even though it still bears the Duchess's name.

Aviation is a major theme in the story of Christchurch between the wars. The very first aerial photograph of the city (page 81) was taken by Leslie Hinge in 1918, and in 1926 the City Council commissioned the city's first vertical aerial survey to help with planning. Henry Wigram kept his Sockburn flying school going after the end of the war, but his efforts to get the government to take it over fell on deaf ears until the Chanak crisis of 1922 and Sir Heaton Rhodes (as Minister of Defence) changed Massey's mind. Wigram's generous gift of £10,000 reduced the cost by a third and led to a change of name: Wigram Aerodrome was New Zealand's first air-force base and the birthplace of the RNZAF.

Sockburn Aerodrome became Wigram Aerodrome in June 1923 when the government finally agreed to take over the pilot-training school established by Henry Wigram during the First World War. This photograph of 1924 shows an assortment of Bristol fighters, Avro 504 Ks and DH4s.

R. P. Moore photograph, Meers collection, CHAC/CM 828

Aerial view of Lyttelton, 1924.
Reclamation work is already well
advanced for the oil-storage area in front
of Naval Point (right). Gladstone Quay
and the coal-loading plant extend (left)
from Officers Point.

CM 12477

'The Bottleneck', Colombo Street,
November 1928, looking south from
Cathedral Square.

CM 3892

90

Above: 'Having a Sun Bath', New Brighton Beach, c. 1920.

S. C. Smith photograph, CM 6160

Below: Papanui Buildings, 1920s, as a Self Help store. Harewood Road on the left. A Perfection ice-cream ('It's a Food, Not a Fad') van is making a delivery of Eskimo pies.

Read collection, CHAC/CM 890

Part of the crowd at Wigram Aerodrome on 11 September 1928 to welcome Charles Kingsford Smith's *Southern Cross* after the first successful trans-Tasman flight.

Litchfield album, CM 16207

Civic reception for the *Southern Cross* crew in Cranmer Square. Kingsford Smith at left, the Mayor (the Reverend J. K. Archer) speaking. Sir Heaton Rhodes (next right), former Minister of Defence, welcomed the aviators on behalf of the government. Archer was a top-polling city councillor and Mayor of Christchurch 1925–31.

CM 16208

Wigram Aerodrome was chosen as the preferred destination of the first successful trans-Tasman flight, by Charles Kingsford-Smith and his crew in their Fokker-F tri-motor *Southern Cross* in September 1928. All-night radio broadcasts alerted the public to their approach, escorted by planes from the flying school, and it seemed as if nearly every motorcar in Christchurch converged on Wigram that morning. A crowd estimated at thirty thousand watched the plane touch down. Sir Heaton Rhodes welcomed Kingsford-Smith on behalf of the government, in a live-broadcast speech, before the crew was whisked away for a civic reception in Cranmer Square. Christchurch had witnessed the dawn of international air travel to New Zealand.

Radio was the great popular medium of this period, after the movies. People had been experimenting with primitive radio sets early in the Great War, but the real growth of enthusiasts' groups came in the early years of peace. The Radio Society of Christchurch was formed in February 1921, and in 1923 it began a regular radio transmission as station 3AC. The Radio Broadcasting Company of New Zealand – the country's first public radio company – was floated in Christchurch in August 1925, and soon became a major force in the medium, eventually owning a chain of YA stations throughout New Zealand. By 1926 radio station 3YA had begun its long career in Christchurch, and its programmes were being printed in the daily newspapers. The tall lattice-work mast on its building in Gloucester Street remained a familiar sight in the city for the next seventy years. In May 1926 Allan Allardyce made the first sports broadcast in New Zealand, from a rugby match at Lancaster Park. He soon pioneered broadcasts of racing, cricket and hockey as well.

Radio plays were an obvious extension of traditional drama to a new medium, and Christchurch had a rich pool of local talent to draw from, thanks largely to the efforts of one charismatic teacher. The energetic James Shelley joined the staff of Canterbury University College in 1920 as New Zealand's first Professor of Education, and over the next sixteen years he made an outstanding contribution to New Zealand drama, adult education and the Country Library Service. He was an actor-director, and led regular play readings for the College Drama Society (as well as giving the first art history lectures at Canterbury). In 1927 he formed the Little Theatre and introduced Christchurch audiences to a stimulating and varied fare. Almost single-handedly he started the renaissance of modern drama in New Zealand, after the early movies had virtually killed off traditional Edwardian theatre companies. Shelley went on to greater things when he became New Zealand's first Director of Broadcasting in 1936. His effect on Christchurch's cultural life had been enormous, and others continued what he had begun. The Canterbury Repertory Theatre Society staged its first production in November 1928.

While music tended to languish in Christchurch in the twenties (apart from ever-enthusiastic brass bands), art enjoyed a renaissance under the leadership of Archibald Nicoll as head of the Art School. A highly accomplished portrait painter, he also encouraged his students to look at the Canterbury landscape with fresh eyes, uncluttered by Northern Hemisphere conventions. By 1926, reviewers were noticing the emergence of a 'Canterbury school' in Christchurch, and in 1927 the formation of 'The Group'. These young painters, including Rita Angus and Olivia Spencer-Bower, had a profound influence on New Zealand painting, and

Sir R. Heaton Rhodes (1861–1956) was born at Purau, namesake son of the pioneer runholder. Educated at Oxford (Brasenose College) he was a notable sportsman and a member of the Christchurch polo team which won the first Savile Cup, 1890. MP for Ellesmere 1899–1925, Minister of Health and Postmaster-General 1912–15, Minister of Defence 1920–26, Knight Commander and Bailiff Grand Cross of the Order of St John. A noted horticulturalist, philatelist and philanthropist, Heaton Rhodes was Canterbury's most-admired public figure when he died.

St John Archives

Christchurch at this time was the undisputed centre of the visual arts in New Zealand, just as its Art School (which introduced the Diploma in Fine Arts in 1929) was long regarded as the best in Australasia.

Christchurch's prosperity was still closely tied to that of Canterbury's farmers, and whenever they sneezed, the city caught a cold; but what happened in the period 1929 to 1936 was rather more like a bout of pneumonia without antibiotics. Export prices fluctuated across the twenties, with sharp falls in 1922 and 1926, but the decline in 1929 was steep after the Wall Street crash, and just kept going down, to reach all-time low levels in 1932–33. Christchurch was hit hardest of New Zealand's main centres by the Depression, and its recovery was slower until the demands of war after 1939 boosted the local economy, especially the manufacturing sector.

These were the notorious 'sugarbag years' of mass unemployment. Between 1931 and 1937 Christchurch's registered unemployed fluctuated between 4,500 and 6,000. The 1936 census gave Christchurch a male unemployment rate of 14.5 per cent, compared with 11.8 in Auckland and 9.5 in Wellington. Yet the official figures did not include men on part-time relief work, working for local bodies. In 1933 Mayor Dan Sullivan said there were at least five thousand men and their families 'deep in poverty' in Christchurch, surviving on charity and relief handouts, and growing their own vegetables in back gardens.

Opposite top: The Christchurch Orchestral Society on 15 April 1930. Besides this professional orchestra, Christchurch had four theatre orchestras during the silent-movie era, giving the city notable depth of instrumental talent to add to its numerous choral societies. But the advent of 'talkies' and radio forced them all into recess during the thirties.

CM 9005

Opposite bottom: Dixon Brothers in Cashel Street were one of the city's best-known butchers, and this impressive display of staff and meats (complete with buffalo head) shows why. The floor was covered in sawdust, swept up and renewed daily.

Dixon collection, CHAC/CM 330

Below: Drainlaying in Jeffreys Road, Bryndwr, November 1928. The Drainage Board managed to complete a major extension of the city's sewerage system to outer suburbs during the twenties, just before the Depression.

Pheloung collection, CHAC/ CM 542

SAVE YOUR MONEY
By purchasing
BEEF. VEAL. PORK.
& our high Grade Small Goods.

The high price of Mutton & Lamb
is caused by the great demand for these
best lines at home.
DIXON BROS

Above: 'Hospital Corner', Riccarton Avenue: Christchurch Public Hospital in the 1930s. Main entrance and administration block on the left, Maids' Quarters on the corner, Nurses' Home (1894) on the right. Not one of these buildings exists today, the last being demolished in the 1980s to make way for the new hospital and medical school.

Canterbury Area Health Board, CHAC/CM 782

Below: Cathedral Square, c. 1930. A typical Christchurch street scene, with trams, motorcars and the inevitable bicycles. The tower of the Crystal Palace cinema in the background remained a city landmark until the 1960s.

Tanner Brothers photograph, CM 3742

Cathedral Square, Christchurch, N.Z.

William Fox, 'Port Lyttelton: Immigrants' luggage disembarking, January 1851'. This shows the jetty and buildings erected by Captain Thomas, and the line of the Bridle Path snaking up the hill beyond.

James Edward FitzGerald, 'The Plain around Christchurch', 1852. Heathcote River in foreground, with wharf and ferry. Ferry Road leads off towards Christchurch in the distance.

James Edward FitzGerald, 'House and Tents occupied by Mr Godley, 1852.' Deans Bush at Riccarton (Putaringamotu) in the background, River Avon in foreground.

CM 5617

Emily W. Harper, 'Christchurch from near Gloucester Street Bridge, 1857.' The Land Office is centre (viewed end-on), W. Guise Brittan's house at left (on the site of the Clarendon Hotel), first St Michael and All Angels' Anglican Church in distance on right, with the vicarage beyond.

Mrs Elizabeth Acland

The Great Hall (or Stone Chamber), Canterbury Provincial Council buildings: Benjamin Mountfort's masterpiece, opened 21 November 1865. William Brassington was the stonemason, and the ceiling was painted by John St Quentin, using Mountfort's stencils. The building was restored and earthquake-proofed in the 1980s.

Photograph: Duncan Shaw-Brown

Sidney Smith, 'Colombo Street, Christchurch, 1884'. View west from the Bank of New Zealand. This is the site later occupied by the United Service Hotel. The Post Office clock tower is at right, New Zealand Insurance building at rear.

Dr John Gosset

Postcard: 'N.Z. International Exhibition, 1906–7, Hagley Park, Christchurch'. Park Terrace and Avon River in foreground. 'Wonderland' amusement park beside Lake Victoria at left. The main entrance faced Kilmore Street.

CM/CHAC

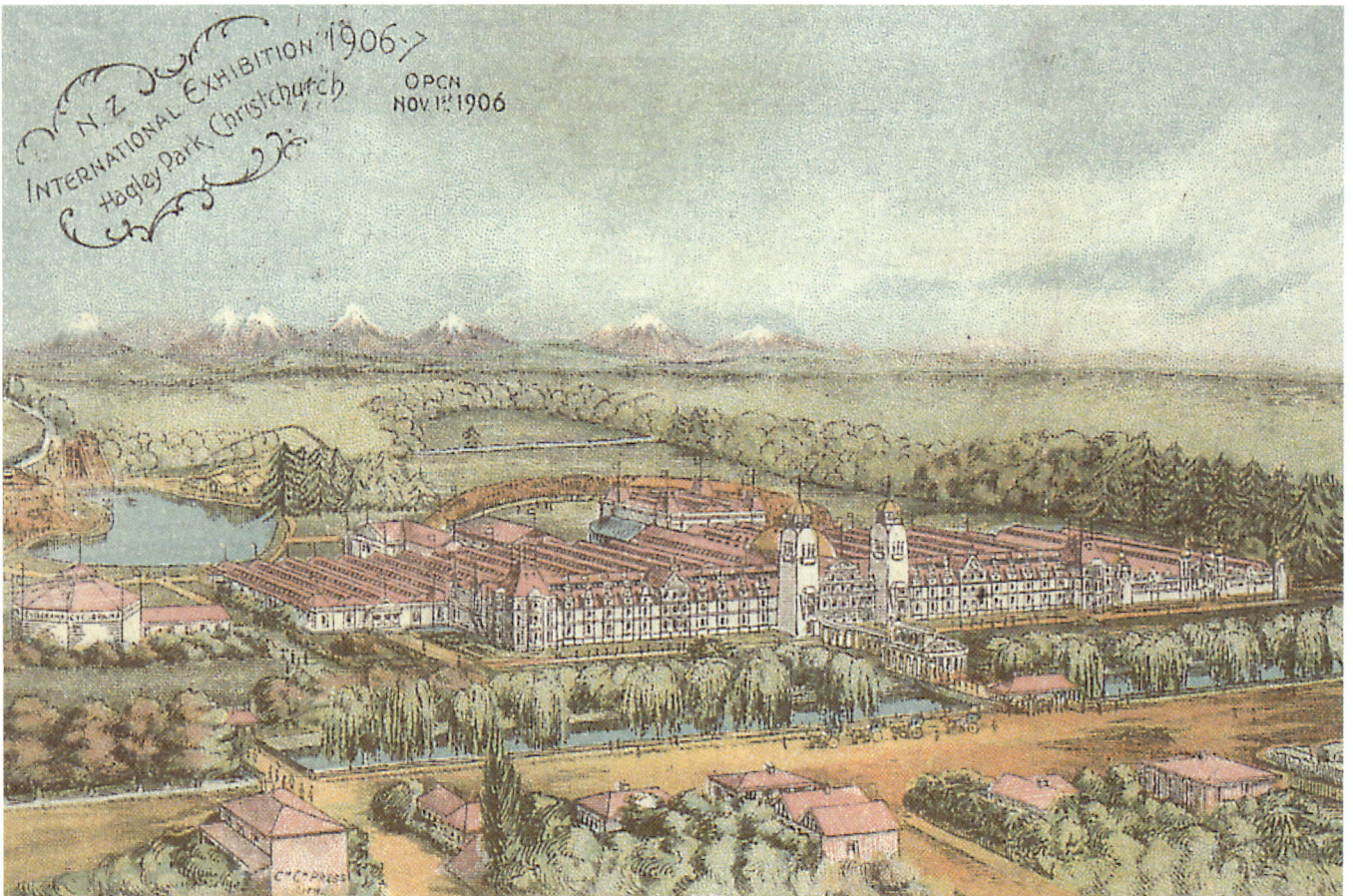

James Fitzgerald, 'High Street, Christchurch: relaying the tram track', 1930s.
CM 16298

James Fitzgerald, 'Cathedral Square', 1944.
CM JF36

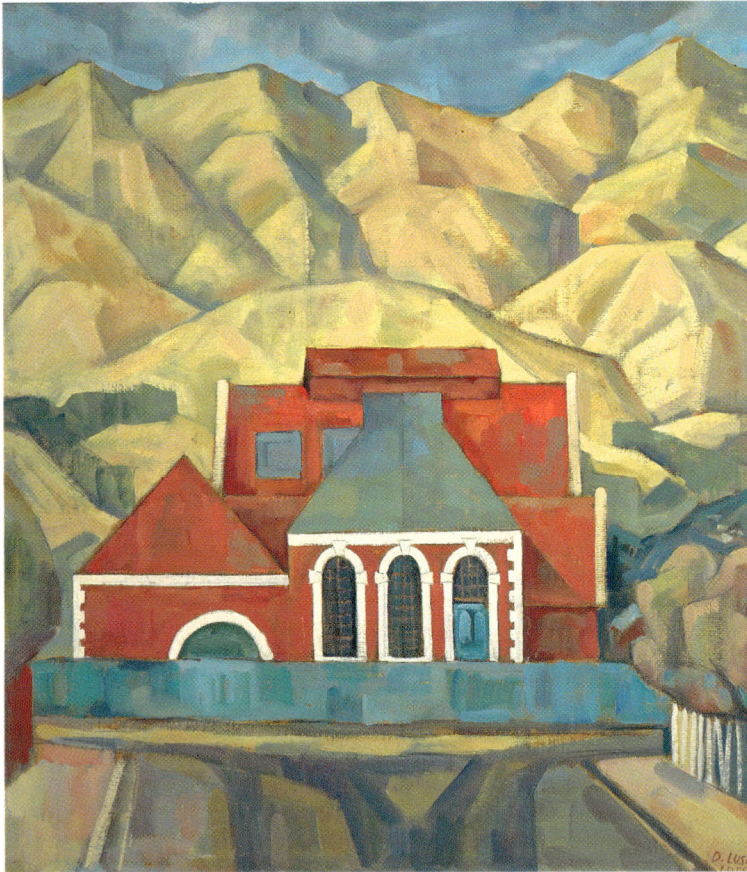

Left: Doris Lusk, 'The Pumping Station', 1958. Still standing, this is Christchurch's first sewage pumping works, built c. 1883 on the Tuam Street / Mathesons Road corner.

Auckland City Art Gallery/Toi o Tamaki, purchased 1968

Below: W. A. Sutton, 'Nor'wester in the Cemetery', 1950. A classic Canterbury icon. The building is the 1860s chapel of the Barbadoes Street Cemetery, now demolished.

Auckland City Art Gallery/Toi o Tamaki, purchased 1954

Past and present: the old Post Office (1879), Cathedral Square, with Telecom Centre (1983).

Victoria Square, looking north, 1999. Captain Cook in his new location, the Town Hall complex (1972) in the middle distance and the Parkroyal Hotel far left.

The restored Peacock Fountain (first erected in 1911) in its new location (1996) beside the Canterbury Museum, near Rolleston Avenue.   Although popular with tourists, its bright colours at first caused some controversy.

John Britten (1950–95), engineer and designer of the revolutionary Britten V 1000 motorcycle, of which only ten were made. A fitting symbol of Christchurch's capacity for technical and entrepreneurial flair.

The Press

Several historians have claimed that Christchurch during the Depression was different from other New Zealand cities; that it escaped the riots of the North Island, and was better organised to look after its unemployed. Because the City Council was controlled by Labour mayors through the whole Depression period, Christchurch is seen as a unique example of Labour 'in office' before the 1935 general election landslide made it the government. It is true that the Christchurch City Council refused to apply the ten per cent cut to the wages of its permanent employees recommended by the Arbitration Court. But recent research has shown conclusively that the Labour council of the Depression years was deeply conservative in financial matters, anxious to avoid any jibes about 'spendthrift socialists'. As a result, Christchurch amassed considerable financial reserves while spending far less than the other main centres on relief work for the unemployed. The council's parsimony forced large numbers of single men to leave Christchurch to work in camps in the country.

Apart from ugly incidents in 1930 and 1931 when the police drew their batons to disperse angry crowds of unemployed men, the worst violence in Christchurch during the Depression was linked to the ten-day tramway strike in May 1932. Faced with falling income, the Tramway Board at first kept afloat by rationing work, but then issued dismissal notices, and the men threatened to strike. Incidents of stone-throwing led the board to cover drivers' windows with wire netting. The worst clash was early on Friday 6 May, as the first cars left the shed in Falsgrave Street. A large crowd of men and a few women tried to stop them, but were charged by a larger number of 'Specials' wearing steel helmets. Unemployed men on relief projects went out in sympathy, and more violence was seen in Cathedral Square that afternoon. A strikebreaker died after being punched in the face, and many others involved in the fracas, including police, were injured.

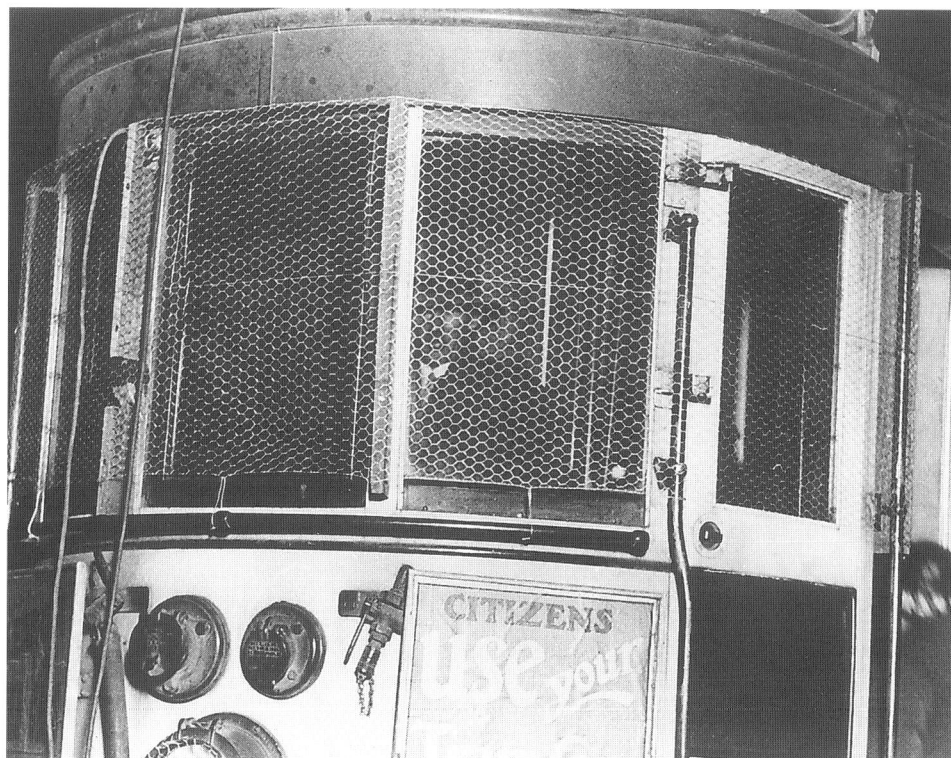

Daniel Giles Sullivan (1882–1947) was born in Waltham, Christchurch, the son of an Irish labourer. A voracious reader, he was largely self-educated and became active in the trade union movement. He was a city councillor 1915–31, topping the poll four times, and was MP for Avon from 1919 until his death. Elected mayor in 1931, he resigned in 1936 after becoming Minister of Industries and Commerce (1935–47) and Minister of Railways (1935–41). His funeral was attended by vast crowds, reflecting his widespread popularity.

Christchurch City Council

Tramway strike, May 1932. Wire mesh protects the windows of a tram against stone-throwers. This was Christchurch's most bitter industrial dispute in this period, with violent clashes between striking unionists and special constables equipped with steel helmets and long wooden batons.

Brittenden collection, CHAC/CM 1179

The Edmonds Band Rotunda (1929), designed by Victor Hean, was one of several notable benefactions to the city between the wars; the Robert McDougall Art Gallery is another. This handsome Italianate crescent was the scene of a Venetian river carnival in January 1935 to mark a royal visit by HRH the Duke of Gloucester. The rotunda was converted into a restaurant in 1987.

Canterbury Museum

Despite the Depression, Christchurch acquired some significant civic landmarks in this period, mostly thanks to private philanthropy. Thomas Edmonds had prospered from small beginnings in Ferry Road making baking powder, and his 1920 factory with its 'Sure to Rise' sign remains a New Zealand icon on the cover of the *Edmonds Cookery Book*. He gave the city a handsome band rotunda and riverside plaza in 1928, and a clock tower near the Madras Street bridge. In 1931 the Bowker fountain in Victoria Square was opened, the cost of which had been bequeathed ten years before. Its coloured-light display has ever since been a feature of Christchurch after dark. In 1928 the will of James Jamieson be-

Victoria Square on a frosty morning. The statue of Captain Cook by local sculptor William Trethewey was donated by a bookmaker, M. F. Barnett, and unveiled on 10 August 1932.

Christchurch Star

98

queathed his notable art collection to the city on condition that it immediately build a gallery to house it: the managing director of Aulsebrook's, Robert McDougall, donated the cost, and the gallery that now bears his name was opened on a site behind the Museum in June 1932. Also opened in 1932 was New Regent Street, on the site of the old Colosseum Hall. It is the only example in New Zealand of a street designed as an entity – in this case in Spanish Mission style.

In 1933 the Godley statue was returned to its original position in the middle of Cathedral Square. This at last resolved the problem of a site for the long-delayed project for a citizens' war memorial, led by George Gould jnr, chairman of the Press Company, Pyne Gould and Guinness and the New Zealand Shipping Company. (He was also a leading stockbreeder and racehorse owner.) Impressed by William Trethewey's Captain Cook statue, Gould's committee commissioned the sculptor to design this memorial, on the site beside the Cathedral vacated by the Godley statue. The design was accepted in 1933 and took four years to complete, but it is arguably the finest group of public statuary in New Zealand. Trethewey based the figures on members of his own family. He was the country's outstanding home-grown sculptor of the early twentieth century, and the Christchurch War Memorial is his masterpiece.

Cathedral Square, 1928, viewed from the north. Crystal Palace cinema lower right, Londontown drapery store lower left. The Rink Stables site (lower right) has been cleared for construction of Hay's department store. Note the Godley statue beside the Cathedral.
RNZAF Museum Wg F22

Denis James Matthews Glover (1912–82) was one of New Zealand's best lyric poets. Journalist, typographer, printer, poet and wit, he won the DSC on D-Day in 1944, commanding a landing craft.

CM 16022

Dame (Edith) Ngaio Marsh (1899–1982), born in Christchurch and a student at the Art School, became an internationally acclaimed writer of detective fiction, publishing thirty novels between 1933 and her death. Her first career was as an actress, touring with professional companies in the 1920s, and her interest in drama led to a parallel career as New Zealand's leading Shakespearian producer and director, achieving professional standards with student casts.

Christchurch Star

New Zealand's literary renaissance between the wars originated at Canterbury University College, where Professor F. Sinclaire and Winston Rhodes edited an independent radical weekly, *Tomorrow*. Many notable New Zealand writers were first published in this journal, including Allen Curnow, Frank Sargeson, R. D. Fairburn, R. A. K. Mason, Robin Hyde and Denis Glover. Glover was one of the liveliest spirits, who helped launch *Canta* as a rival student journal to the staid *College Review*. In 1935 he co-founded The Caxton Press, which continued to publish the work of young writers and poets who had appeared in *Tomorrow*. They were throwing off the colonial conventions of an English-based literature and exploring the emerging identity of New Zealand. Glover's superb typography, and the assembled talents of his writers, poets and illustrators, made Christchurch the country's literary capital in the 1930s.

Indirectly, the city's reputation was enhanced by the success overseas of Ngaio Marsh, a former Art School student who had exhibited with The Group. She achieved great success throughout the English-speaking world as a writer of detective fiction after the publication of her first novel, *A Man Lay Dead*, in 1934. Marsh was acclaimed as the new Agatha Christie and went on to publish dozens of successful novels. Her work as a drama producer after her return to Christchurch made her a female counterpart to Professor Shelley as a 'Renaissance figure'.

The city's manufacturing sector suffered along with the rest of the region's economy during the 1930s Depression, but then made a strong recovery from a solid base in engineering, clothing and food products. Several Christchurch firms began to take advantage of new materials and technologies. In 1936 H. C. Urlwin began to manufacture New Zealand's first moulded-plastic products at a factory in Waltham Road, and soon added electrical appliances. A big fire in August 1939 set them back temporarily, and other rivals soon appeared, but the plastics and electrical sector has remained strong in Christchurch ever since. Alhough Christchurch never became a centre for motor-vehicle manufacturing, it helped to provide what they rode on, and many other items made from rubber. George Skellerup had started the Para Rubber Company in 1910, selling bicycle tyres and imported rubber goods. In the late 1920s Para acquired agencies for motorcar tyres, and exhibited widely at agricultural shows. In 1933 Skellerup set up the Latex Rubber Company to make waterproof clothing, and in 1939 both the Marathon Rubber Footwear Company to make gumboots and the Empire Rubber Mills to manufacture milkware. By then, Skellerup's Woolston factories had become the heart of New Zealand's rubber industry.

Retailing also began to pick up again in the mid-thirties. Old established firms like Ballantyne's, Beath's and the DIC had to narrow their profit margins to cope with competition from the likes of Drayton Jones. Hay's had started in 1928 as the subsidiary of a large Auckland firm, but when it folded in 1933 J. L. Hay formed a public company with Canterbury shareholders to build a new store in Gloucester Street, on the old Rink Stables site. Hay's ('the friendly store') became one of the South Island's leading department stores, with innovative advertising and a children's league to foster customer loyalty. (Whenever a circus came to town, Hay's would hire its elephants to advertise a sale.)

Another major Christchurch store grew from small beginnings in Ferry Road in 1926. Lesley Beaumont Miller was an Australian who had moved to Christ-

100

Interior of Londontown Drapery, Colombo Street, 1920s. Christchurch has always been a major centre for clothing manufacture, and this was one of many retail shops in the inner city in the 1920s employing young women in large numbers. The name reflects Christchurch's pride in its English origins.

Bolland collection, CHAC/CM 95

The Christchurch gasworks, c. 1930. Coal gas was produced here from 1864 until 1982, after which the site was completely cleared, including large quantities of contaminated soil.

S. W. Perkins photograph, CHAC/CM 873

church from Greymouth. He then set up a retail shop and clothing factory in the old Strange's building on the corner of Lichfield and and High Streets in 1930, and bought a woollen mill in Invercargill to supply his shop. As 'the worker's friend' Miller's grew during the Depression by selling well-made clothing at low prices. In 1939 they moved into a new five-storey bulding in Tuam Street, which remains one of Christchurch's best examples of Modernist architecture. (It also boasted the first escalator in the South Island.) Next door, Lichfield shirts were made by one of the city's expanding clothing manufacturers of the late thirties.

Anderson's engineering works remained on its Lichfield Street site in the city well into this period, though all its heavy steelwork was done elsewhere. By the late thirties a new plant was being built in Woolston, which saw huge expansion after 1939. Scott Brothers had long since ceased to make steam locomotives, and diversified their output from coal ranges to electric ovens, employing over a hundred men on this new line in 1935. Duncans', Andrews and Beaven, and Booth Macdonald continued to make agricultural machinery, and Steel Brothers were outstripping Boon and Company as the city's leading coachbuilders. Despite the Depression, which drove many small firms to the wall, Christchurch's major companies mostly survived intact, bruised but not beaten.

As the Depression slowly eased, the city welcomed some notable visitors. George Bernard Shaw gave a memorable nationwide broadcast from Christchurch in April 1934, and the Duke of Gloucester was entertained by a 'Venetian river carnival' on the Avon in January 1935. Lord Bledisloe, one of New Zealand's best-loved governors-general, was a regular visitor to Canterbury A&P shows. Two musicians of world renown who visited Christchurch in 1935 were Percy Grainger and Yehudi Menuhin (the latter already a famous violinist at seventeen). An influential visitor who came to stay was the Austrian refugee Karl Popper, who lectured at Canterbury University College from 1937 to 1945. While in Christchurch he wrote *The Open Society and its Enemies*, which established his reputation as one of the world's leading philosophers of science.

102

Christchurch was improving its contacts with the outside world in more than philosophy. In December 1935 the city council finally gave up its dreams of a flying-boat base on the Estuary and bought a large block of land at Harewood for a city airport. The following January, Union Airways inaugurated the first regular passenger service by air between the North and South Islands with DH 89 Dominie aircraft. Air travel grew rapidly in popularity for those who could afford it, but most Christchurch people travelling to Wellington still took the overnight ferry from Lyttelton.

In politics, Canterbury's farmer Prime Minister George Forbes (1930–35) has not had a good press from historians, and was reviled by the unemployed for his overly cautious conservative approach to the unprecedented problems of the Depression. Much more popular in Christchurch was Elizabeth McCombs, who became New Zealand's first woman MP when she was elected to replace her late husband in the Lyttelton seat in 1933. Her health was not good, however, and overwork may have hastened her death in 1935. The seat stayed in the family, though, with the election of her son T. H. (later Sir Terence) McCombs. Christchurch South (which included Sydenham) remained a Labour stronghold throughout this period with Ted Howard as its MP (1919–39), but Christchurch North became another family fiefdom in 1935 when Henry Holland retired and his son S. G. (later Sir Sidney) Holland polled the highest vote of any National candidate in the country, despite the Labour landslide of that election. Dan Sullivan and H. T. (Tim) Armstrong were Christchurch MPs who now became Cabinet ministers.

Addington Railway Workshops, 1934. Though no longer making steam locomotives, this was one of the city's largest engineering works, employing hundreds of men and apprentices. Like the gasworks, this site was completely cleared in the 1980s, except for the concrete water tower. Woods' Mill grain-drying sheds in the foreground.

Christchurch Star

103

Elizabeth Reid McCombs (1873–1935), New Zealand's first woman MP, was also one of New Zealand's first woman JPs and only the second woman elected to the Christchurch City Council. Her husband, James McCombs, was Labour MP for Lyttelton (1913–33). She held the seat with a large majority until her death, and was succeeded by her son Terence (1935–51), later Sir Terence McCombs, Minister of Education, 1947–49.

Christchurch Star

On the eve of the Second World War, Christchurch was still recovering from the effects of the Depression, but outsiders often saw it as a solidly prosperous place, and could point to a variety of new public buildings to support their argument. The Municipal Electricity Building on the corner of Armagh and Manchester Streets (1939) was a prime example. But many parts of the city's fabric and infrastructure were looking shabby and neglected. Roads were a prime source of complaint. Cyclists had to be wary not only of tramlines but of the deep potholes that developed alongside them. One of the worst arterial routes was Riccarton Road, because Riccarton Borough never spent enough on its upkeep, and its ratepayers strenuously resisted any rates increases. Spreydon and Woolston had joined the city in 1921, followed by Bromley and Papanui in 1923, leaving Riccarton isolated as an independent borough well within the metropolitan district. Sumner and New Brighton were far enough distant to manage their own affairs, but Riccarton remained a problem, as did the growing suburbs on land controlled by Waimairi and Paparua Counties.

Even so, Christchurch people in the thirties somehow contrived to enjoy themselves. Crowds flocked to Lancaster Park in the winter, whatever the weather, to watch the rugby – especially if it was a Ranfurly Shield match – and to the races at Riccarton, Addington or New Brighton. (The first Inter-Dominion trotting meeting in New Zealand was held at Addington in April 1938.) In summer, the beaches at Sumner and New Brighton attracted thousands to swim or sunbathe. Surf lifesaving clubs grew in popularity in this period.

If all else failed, there was always the garden to tend. These two decades

Opposite top: DIC Social Club Revue, c. 1939. Entertainment in the thirties was heavily influenced by American films and music.

Yeatman collection, CHAC/CM 283

Opposite bottom: Reese Brothers' Addington Service Station, c. 1938, with an assortment of brands to choose from, and oil in glass bottles.

Baker collection, CHAC/CM 311

Right: Shopping was never complete without a welcome interlude for morning or afternoon tea. All the larger department stores had their own tearooms, but the Quality Inn, pictured here, was one of many small tearooms that dotted inner Christchurch between the wars.

CM 6902

IN THE BOTANICAL GARDENS, CHRISTCHURCH, N.Z.

The Peacock fountain was funded from a £500 bequest to the Christchurch Beautifying Association by a leading businessman and politician, the Hon. J. T. Peacock (1827–1906). Despite suggestions for a local design, the fountain ordered was Design No. 38 from the catalogue of the Coalbrookdale Iron Works in England. The fountain fell into disrepair and was dismantled in 1949. It was restored on a new site in 1996 (see colour section).

CM/CHAC 526

were a golden age for the Canterbury Horticultural Society, under the benign presidency of Sir Heaton Rhodes, who was now the province's much-loved elder statesman. The society gave inspiration and encouragement to thousands of home gardeners, reinforcing Christchurch's image as the 'Garden City'. Its journal (taken over in 1927 from the Beautifying Association) was entitled *The City Beautiful*. The City Council also actively promoted Christchurch's 'green' aspect, developing numerous suburban parks from old shingle pits that had been filled as rubbish dumps. The rivers were tamed in this period, with rows of willows and trimmed lawns, which gave a restful alternative to the rows of look-alike bungalows, power poles draped with wires, and roads full of potholes that marred the city's suburbs. It all looked very pleasant from a distance.

CHAPTER SIX

Conformist Christchurch
1940 – 1959

Uniforms are a visible key to understanding these two decades. Uniforms were everywhere. First, the khaki of soldiers, the dark blue of sailors and the lighter blue of airmen as Christchurch farewelled its sons to fight in the Second World War. Each of the brass bands that farewelled them had its own distinctive uniform. Uniforms implied rank and a chain of command: people in uniform gave orders, or obeyed them. This was an authoritarian era, of clearly defined public and private spheres. Parades and processions became a common sight in the city's streets, especially of young airmen, as hundreds of pilots for the RNZAF were trained at Wigram and Harewood in the 1940s. Then came women in uniform, as WAACs or WAAFs, or as tram conductors and guards on trains, to enable more men to join the forces.

Recruits for the Fourth Reinforcement, 2NZEF, march across the Bridge of Remembrance on 3 October 1940, on their way to Burnham Camp for uniforms, weapons and endless drill.

Green and Hahn photograph, CM 3980

Even after the war, shortages of material prolonged the drab greys and browns of wartime civilian clothes. Grey flannel trousers and tweed sports jackets became almost a peacetime uniform for men, along with the ubiquitous grey felt hat. Everyone wore hats in public, including high-school pupils, who also had to wear uniforms. Women would not dream of 'going into town' without hat, gloves and handbag, and, of course, nylon stockings and lipstick, two of the most-missed adornments of the war years. The Korean War (1950–54) brought back compulsory military training for young men, and the cadet scheme meant that even schoolboys wore khaki on certain days of the week. This was a period of conformity as well as uniformity, both products of the war years. Well into the fifties Christchurch was in many ways a regimented city, constrained by rules and regulations.

The city's war effort in the 1940s was different in many ways from that of the Great War. Christchurch still packaged and processed the products of the Canterbury Plains, but now its manufacturing sector was equally important, especially in plastics, electrical goods and motor assembly. The city produced thousands of uniforms and greatcoats for the armed forces, as well as boots and steel helmets, grenade casings and other munitions. Fund-raising for the war effort at first went very slowly in Christchurch. Just as the first year of the European war was dubbed the 'phoney war', so too in Christchurch it had an air of unreality, of something too far away to cause much local concern. In 1939 there was not the same wave of patriotic feeling as there had been in 1914.

But the war became more of a reality early in January 1940, with the departure from Lyttelton of the First Echelon of Canterbury troops for the Second NZEF. Three more echelons followed, in April, August and October 1940. Christchurch's Emergency Precautions Scheme (EPS) had swung into being as soon as war was declared, and its first air-raid exercise was held on 19 January. Leaflets were scattered across the city asking, 'If this were a bomb, where would you be?' People were urged to join the Home Guard or contribute to the Red Cross. Petrol rationing started on 1 February 1940, a few days after the city council had voted to ban pacifist meetings for the duration. A crowd had threatened to throw a pacifist clergyman into the Avon River for his 'unpatriotic views'.

By early 1941 the EPS and Home Guard organisations in Christchurch were reaching high standards of efficiency, and blackout exercises were much improved. Home Guard enrolments reached 5,500 in March 1941. Petrol shortages led some owners to install bulky gas bags on their car roofs, fed by wood-to-gas converters. The whole city smiled in October at the news that a local man, Charles Upham, had been awarded the Victoria Cross for his bravery on Crete. The A&P Show in November (the last for four years) was smaller than usual, but the races that week attracted their heaviest betting since 1921.

Most of the war news had been gloomy thus far, after the fall of France and the narrow victory of the Battle of Britain in 1940. London had suffered nightly bombing raids in the Blitz, and Germany had invaded Denmark and Norway. New Zealand troops had shared in spectacular successes against the Italians in North Africa, but were then sent to fight rearguard actions in Greece and Crete, where many were captured. Unlike the Great War, in which relatively few New Zealanders were captured, the Second World War produced lists of prisoners of war almost as long as the casualty lists.

Sir Ernest Herbert Andrews (1873–1961). Mayor of Christchurch 1941–50 and a member of the City Council 1919–50, he established the printing firm Andrews, Baty Ltd in 1907. He was EPS District Commander during the war, and a long-serving member of the Education and Tramway Boards.

CHAC/CM 50

Opposite top: Woolston and Bromley after snow and heavy rain in August 1941. Linwood Avenue (before trees) runs diagonally towards the Estuary. Ruru Lawn Cemetery and the Crematorium (1940) centre and left.

CM 5401

Bottom: New state houses in Riccarton, 8 December 1941. Power poles were placed between back yards to give the streets a clean and uncluttered appearance.

Green and Hahn photograph, MED collection, CHAC/CM 1006

Robert Mafeking Macfarlane (1901–81) was Mayor of Christchurch 1938–41 and MP for Christchurch South 1939–46. After war service, he became MP for Christchurch Central (1946–69), Mayor again (1950–58), and Deputy Mayor 1971–74.

Christchurch Star

The war suddenly changed from a distant anxiety to a very immediate threat when Japan bombed Pearl Harbor early in December, and then unleashed its lightning conquest of South-East Asia. A Japanese invasion of Australia and New Zealand now seemed only a matter of time, and the first attack was expected to come from the air, by carrier-based bombers. Air-raid shelters were dug in Cathedral Square, and slit trenches were dug in Cranmer and Latimer Squares, while EPS personnel visited city firms to check on their precautions. Plans to evacuate women and children to the countryside were prepared, and many Christchurch householders began to dig shelters in their back yards. The National Reserve was mobilised for home defence, and hundreds now applied to join the Home Guard. It was a very quiet Christmas in Christchurch in 1941. The rapid Japanese advances, the sinking of the British battleships *Repulse* and *Prince of Wales*, and the big casualty lists from Greece and Crete made even the optimists more than a little glum.

The fall of Singapore in February 1942 intensified the fear of attack and invasion by Japan. Although America had joined the war, there seemed to be very little to stop the Japanese advance. EPS exercises in the city in March and April involved the Home Guard, fire and ambulance services, and the blackout was strictly enforced. Most people just stayed at home in the evenings, listening nervously to the news on the radio. Fund-raising now went ahead briskly; by April Christchurch had raised £293,000 in the 'Bonds for Bombers' campaign. Deeper air-raid shelters were built in Cathedral Square, using logs from the city council's pine plantations. A fire at the Public Library on 2 May was promptly put out by an EPS team stationed opposite in the YMCA. By July the city had 5,570 fire watchers on nightly duty, awaiting the first Japanese air raid. News of a raid on Sydney Harbour by Japanese midget submarines in May seemed to bring the war to Christchurch's doorstep. Sumner became something of a garri-

Air-raid shelters in an MED yard between Armagh and Gloucester Streets, 1942.

S. Webb photograph, CHAC/CM 1025

110

son town, housing the families of men and women serving in the coastal batteries and anti-aircraft sites around Godley Head and Lyttelton Harbour.

Several top-secret construction projects were pushed ahead by the government. At Lyttelton, two deep tunnels were cut into the rock behind the oil-storage tanks, intended to hold enough fuel to replenish several battleships. An extensive underground operations headquarters was dug under the Cashmere estate, with an access tunnel to the homestead. If the Japanese invaded the North Island, the government and military command would be relocated to Christchurch. Out on the plains near Dunsandel, three huge grass runways were levelled to accommodate American Superfortress bombers.

These major projects were never finished. The tide of war had turned by June 1942, after the great naval battles of the Coral Sea and Midway, and the threat of invasion receded. The tunnels were sealed, and blackout restrictions were eased in December.

Cathedral Square in wartime, 1943, looking remarkably peaceful. Note the 'Food for Britain' banner on the tram shelter in the foreground.

Frank McGregor photograph, CM 5131

Harewood Aerodrome was officially opened as a city council civil airport in May 1940, but was soon after taken over as RNZAF Base Harewood. Hundreds of pilots were trained here and at Wigram during the Second World War.

Stan McKay photograph, CM 11959

While war news continued to dominate the newspapers, some local issues caught the headlines from time to time. The election of Christchurch North MP Sidney Holland as leader of the National Party was a matter of great local interest, as was his withdrawal from the War Cabinet in October 1942 over the Labour government's leniency towards striking miners and freezing workers. The death of long-serving Christchurch East MP H. R. (Tim) Armstrong in November that year caused a by-election, but Miss Mabel Howard held the seat for Labour in February 1943. Robert Macfarlane returned safely from overseas

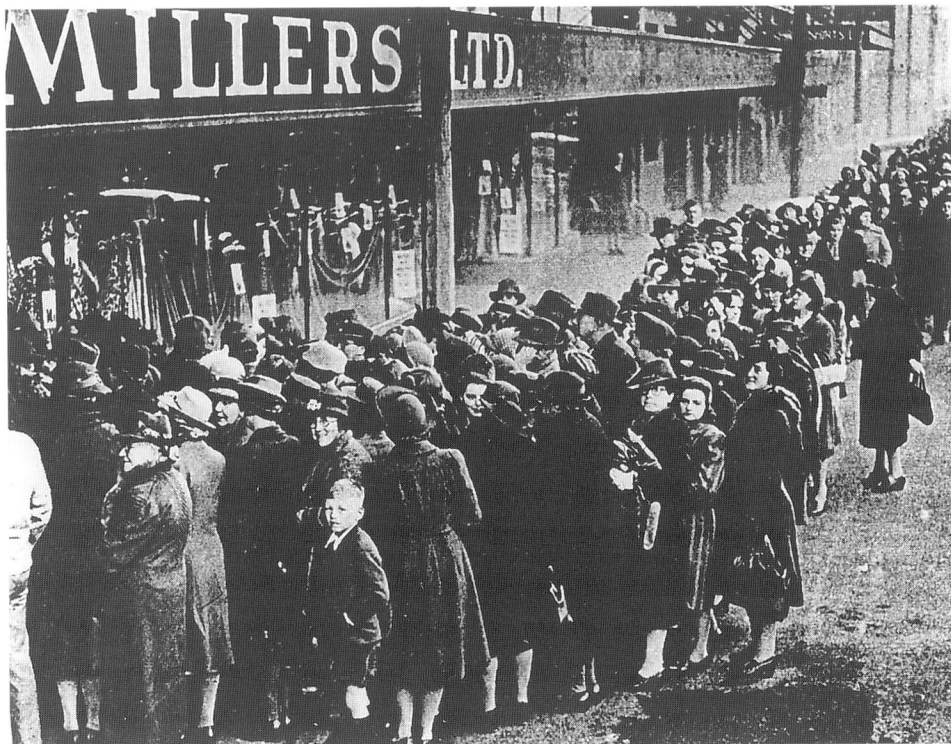

When Miller's store advertised a special shipment of cotton towels in 1944, the queue that formed next morning stretched around the corner and halfway down Manchester Street. Such was the shortage of many imported goods during wartime.

Reg Miller collection, CM 97/86

112

service in time to be re-elected as Member for Christchurch South in September 1943. But the local body elections of 1944 saw a big swing to the right, and heavy defeats for Labour candidates. George Manning was the only Labour councillor to retain his place. Ernest Andrews was re-elected mayor, and James Hay topped the poll for the Citizens' Association, probably thanks to his prominent role in the National Savings campaign. Ron Guthrey, at twenty-eight, was the youngest councillor; he had lost a leg and won the MC in North Africa.

By late 1943 the invasion crisis had long passed and the city's air-raid shelters were filled in. Rationing was eased and the Italian surrender in September brought a cheerful crowd to celebrate in Cathedral Square. The government then reminded everyone that such celebrations were premature, as the war was not yet won. (The city council reinforced the mood of seriousness by banning two-piece swimsuits from Christchurch beaches.) Early in 1944 the Lyttelton Naval Auxiliary Patrol was disbanded, a clear sign that the danger of invasion had eased, and on 25 April the first Dawn Parade was held on Anzac Day in Christchurch, before the main parade and service in the King Edward Barracks.

The war in Europe finally ended in May 1945, and VE Day was celebrated in Christchurch with much impromptu singing and dancing in the streets. The crowd that gathered in Cathedral Square was the largest seen there since 1918. Two months later the city experienced its heaviest recorded snowfall. After a day of warm nor'west gales on 13 July, the city woke on Saturday to find itself blanketed in white, under clear blue skies. The snow was as deep as 30 centimetres in the central city, and took nearly a week to melt. The city's heaviest frost (−7°C) was recorded on 18 July. Schools and shops remained closed, and communications were seriously disrupted by blocked roads and railways, and fallen telephone lines. Many Christchurch people remembered 1945 for the 'Great Snow' as much as for the end of the war.

Hastened by the dropping of atomic bombs on Hiroshima and Nagasaki, Japan's surrender on 15 August was unexpected and anti-climactic. The crowds celebrating VJ Day were smaller but seemed happier, as victory also meant peace

Mabel Howard (1893–1972) was New Zealand's first woman Cabinet minister, in 1947. The daughter of Labour MP Ted Howard (Christchurch South, 1919–39) she was secretary of the Canterbury General Labourers' Union before entering Parliament in a by-election in 1943. She was MP for Sydenham 1946–69 with the largest majority in the country, and Minister of Social Security and Child Welfare in the Second Labour Government, 1957–60.

Christchurch Star

One of Christchurch's heaviest recorded falls of snows occurred in July 1945. This shows Oxford Terrace as the thaw began.

Green and Hahn photograph, MED collection, CHAC/CM 1078

Right: WAAFs march along Worcester
Street on their way to VJ Day
celebrations at Hagley Park.

Bate collection, CHAC/CM

Below: The real end of the Second
World War only came with the surrender
of Japan on VJ Day, celebrated in
Christchurch on 15 August 1945. This is
the crowd in Colombo Street, with
onlookers on the fire escape of the
United Service Hotel.

Stan McKay photograph, CM 13114

114

this time. Already many Christchurch soldiers and airmen who had been prisoners of war in Europe were returning home. Easily the most famous of these was Captain Charles Upham, who had spent the last years of the war imprisoned in Colditz. The announcement of a bar to his VC in September gave deep satisfaction in Christchurch.

The end of the war and the return of many thousands of servicemen placed great strain on the city's housing stock. A large number of state houses had been built during the war in Riccarton, Spreydon and Shirley, but demand far exceeded supply, and former air-force barracks at Harewood were converted into temporary housing for families awaiting a state house. These families were thus well placed to witness the first regular overseas airline service from New Zealand, when the Lancastrian *City of London* left Harewood for Sydney. Air travel had brought Christchurch closer to the rest of the world, and some famous people as visitors after the war: Lord and Lady Mountbatten in 1946 and Field Marshal Bernard Montgomery in 1947. But the post-war years in Christchurch were soon overshadowed by the city's worst-ever blaze, the Ballantyne's fire of 18 November 1947.

This disaster occurred in Show Week, when the city was full of visitors and shoppers. A smouldering basement fire suddenly escaped the fire brigade's control and raced through thin partitions into the upper floors, where accumulated smoke and fumes ignited in a 'flash-over' that engulfed the whole building within minutes. Ballantyne's had no sprinklers or alarm system, and the management had delayed evacuation, thinking the basement fire was under control.

Charles Hazlitt Upham (1908–94), born in Christchurch and educated at Christ's College, was New Zealand's outstanding soldier of the Second World War, winning the Victoria Cross for his gallantry on Crete in May 1941, and a Bar for his bravery at Ruweisat Ridge in July 1942. After the war he became a sheepfarmer in North Canterbury.
Christchurch Star

Ballantyne's department store, corner of Cashel and Colombo Streets, the day after New Zealand's worst fire disaster, in which forty-one staff died.
Wenborn collection, CHAC/CM 18

This delay proved fatal for forty-one of the staff, most of whom were trapped upstairs beyond the reach of the fire brigade's ladders. All the customers and most of the three hundred staff simply fled into the surrounding streets while passers-by gazed with astonishment at the mounting inferno. Off-duty servicemen, along with many civilians, helped with the hoses, and thousands of gallons of water were pumped into the blazing shell, but the fire was far too large and intense to be controlled. The pillar of smoke could be seen all over the city, and many people rushed into town to see what was happening. Out in the suburbs, charred dockets and papers later descended, having been sucked up to a great height by the heat of the fire.

Next day, as the gutted shell cooled, servicemen helped recover the remains of the victims. The fire had become world news, as a crew from the National Film Unit happened to be in Christchurch that afternoon, and its footage was later seen in many countries. Because the bodies had been burned beyond recognition, it was decided to hold joint funeral services and a collective public burial in a mass grave at the Ruru Lawn Cemetery. This was certainly the largest funeral in the city's history, attended by the Prime Minister and many other dignitaries. The route was lined by thousands of mourners. In a close-knit community such as Christchurch was at that time, everyone could claim to know someone who had known the victims or their families. The Ballantyne's fire has remained a landmark of sadness in the city's history, as unforgettable for those alive at the time as the 1906 Exhibition.

Christchurch Railway Station and goods yard, about 1952. Moorhouse Avenue at left, gasworks in the smoky distance. Centre left is the old suburban passenger platform linked by overbridge to the main platform. Scarcely anything in this view has survived; even the gasworks have gone.

Stan McKay photograph, CM 6573

Manchester Street, looking south from the MED building, c. 1950. The New Zealand Express building (1906) now has a tall companion. The white State Insurance building (right) was opened in 1935. Designed by Cecil Wood in Art Deco style, it had Maori motifs in its interior and exterior decoration.

Christchurch Star

Christchurch had a number of pie carts over the years; this is the one in Hereford Street about 1952. After the movies or a dance or late-night party, it was just the place for a quick hot snack and cup of tea.

Ritchie collection, CHAC/CM 1068

117

The Ballantyne's fire completely overshadowed local body elections scheduled for the following day, but not the royal wedding in London on 20 November. Ernest Andrews was re-elected mayor for a third term, and James Hay repeated his 1944 performance by topping the council poll, ahead of George Manning. Grim photos of the ruins of Ballantyne's store and the civic funeral were offset to some extent by large celebratory photos of the wedding of Princess Elizabeth and Philip Mountbatten, reinforcing Christchurch's prevailing mood of Empire loyalty and 'Englishness'.

Although the war had interrupted Christchurch's 'literary renaissance' of the 1930s, associated with The Caxton Press, the city had not been a total cultural desert. In June 1948 Ngaio Marsh was awarded an OBE for services to literature and drama, recognising not only her international reputation as a crime writer but also her productions for the University drama society during the war. Her 1943 *Hamlet* in modern dress, with music by Douglas Lilburn, remains a landmark in New Zealand's theatre history. On the literary front, Charles Brasch established the journal *Landfall* in 1947, published by Caxton, and it soon rose above all its rivals to become New Zealand's leading literary journal of the next three decades.

The forties closed with the National MP for Fendalton, Sidney Holland, becoming the Prime Minister. Christchurch businessmen now felt assured of a more sympathetic hearing from government than they had had during more than a decade of Labour in power. The city's employment prospects also brightened with the opening of the new Firestone factory in Papanui, which produced the first New Zealand-made tyres in 1949. The first Lady Wigram Trophy Race was held at the aerodrome in 1949. This became for several decades the country's major car-racing event, attracting huge crowds and cars and drivers from all over New Zealand. Also opened in 1949 was the Sign of the Takahe on Cashmere Hill, the 'jewel in the crown' of Harry Ell's dream for a Summit Road linking elegant stone tea-houses. It has remained a distinctive city landmark, giving visitors their best view of the Southern Alps.

Christchurch was the scene of carefully planned festivities and commemorative events in December 1950 which recalled the foundation of the Canterbury settlement a hundred years before. The most notable invited guest was the

Sir Sidney Holland (1893–1961), Prime Minister of New Zealand 1949–57, was the son of Henry Holland, who was Mayor of Christchurch, 1912–19 and MP for Christchurch North, 1925–35. He was electorate organiser for his father, and retained the seat in 1935. He served in the War Cabinet, and as Prime Minister abolished the Legislative Council and dealt firmly with the 1951 Waterfront Dispute.

Christchurch Star

Opposite: Colombo Street in 1945, viewed from Moorhouse Avenue. The large white building centre distance is the Post Office Savings Bank in Hereford Street, opened in 1941. Most of the rooftops in the middle distance belong to Whitcombe and Tombs' printing works, a site now occupied by the South City Mall.
Brittenden collection, CHAC/CM 1160

Left: Perhaps the most memorable of the shop displays to mark Canterbury's Centennial was this group of larger-than-lifesize Pilgrims on the single-storey rebuilt Ballantyne's store, complete with tussock. Christchurch's awareness of its English origins peaked in the early fifties.
Frank McGregor photograph, CM 3037

Archbishop of Canterbury, Dr Fisher, who presided over a vast Thanksgiving Service in Cathedral Square on Sunday, 17 December, attended by twenty thousand citizens. According to *The Press*, 'Canterbury gave praise for a settlement built on sure Christian foundations.' Lyttelton had held its main celebrations the day before, with a restored sailing ship enacting the role of the *Charlotte Jane*, landing descendants of the Pilgrims in rowing boats. On the Monday, Christchurch witnessed one of the biggest street processions the city has ever seen. Sixty-nine decorated floats celebrating the theme 'One Hundred Years of Progress' took a circuitous route through the central city, along streets lined with an estimated two hundred thousand people — almost the entire city population. The other major event of 18 December was the Prime Minister's dedication of Harewood as New Zealand's first international airport. Holland declared it 'a great day for Christchurch, for Canterbury, and for New Zealand in general'. Two large aircraft arrived from Australia to mark the occasion.

Ilam, 1950, looking west: future site of the University of Canterbury. Clyde Road in foreground, Creyke Road at right; Ilam School at left beside Ilam Road; carpet factory beyond beside Waimairi Road; Yaldhurst Road and part of Riccarton Racecourse in distance, upper left. In addition to the University buildings, housing now covers nearly all of the land in this photograph.

V. C. Browne photograph, 162

Left: Lancaster Park, one Saturday afternoon in the late fifties. This was the golden age of Ranfurly Shield inter-provincial rugby. For a few extra shillings, you could sit on planks in the Enclosure and be deafened by the roar of the Embankment crowd.

Stan McKay photograph, CM

Below: After the match: Moorhouse Avenue, beside the gasworks, as the crowd leaves Lancaster Park. During the match, buses and cars would be parked bumper to bumper along the middle of this as-yet-treeless avenue.

Frank McGregor photograph, CM

Aviation now became a major theme in the city's development. In October 1953 Harewood was the finishing point for the world's 'last great air race', from London to Christchurch. This had been the brainchild of a local businessman and aviator, Hume Christie, whose efforts had won government-level support in Britain and Australia. The death of King George VI in February 1952 had brought his daughter to the throne as Queen Elizabeth II, and a new wave of patriotic sentiment to greet the 'new Elizabethan age' had swept around the Empire, now becoming known as the Commonwealth. Elizabeth had been due to visit New Zealand, but the tour had been postponed until after her coronation on 2 June. That spectacular event had been further enhanced by the conquest of Mount Everest, the world's highest mountain, by the New Zealander Ed Hillary and his Sherpa guide Tensing Norgay on 29 May. The air race occurred in a context of heightened awareness of New Zealand's place in the Commonwealth, and its links to Britain.

The royal tour of January 1954 must rank with the 1950 Centennial celebrations as one of the city's greatest events, both in terms of the crowds drawn onto the streets and the impression it made on all those who witnessed it. This was the first visit to New Zealand of a reigning British monarch, and the fact that the Queen was a beautiful young mother added enormously to public interest in the tour. Schoolchildren lined the route, waving little Union Jacks and

Opposite top: 'The Bottleneck', 1954. Intersection of Colombo, High and Hereford Streets. United Service Hotel on the left, old Bank of New Zealand on the right.

Frank McGregor photograph, CM 11232

Opposite bottom: Aerial view of central Christchurch, 22 December 1956, looking west across the Avon River towards North Hagley Park. Victoria Square (centre) and the river bank (foreground) are now shaded by an abundance of mature trees.

Star Sun photograph, CM 15397

Below: The royal visit of January 1954 brought out the bunting and flags in great abundance. Here is the display on Miller's department store, Tuam Street. This building is now the Civic Offices.

Biggs collection, CHAC/CM 14925

New Zealand flags; an estimated hundred and fifty thousand people saw the Queen on the day of her ceremonial drive through the city. Although other royal visits were to follow (the Queen Mother came to Christchurch in 1958), the 1954 tour made the most lasting impression, reinforcing the sense of English identity in Christchurch conveyed by the Centennial and the 1953 air race.

Large crowds were also attracted to rugby matches at Lancaster Park in the 1950s, which were often preceded by a procession of floats and brass bands through the city. But the Ranfurly Shield match of 28 August 1954 (Canterbury and Waikato drew, 6–6) was completely overshadowed by the city's most sensational murder trial. Two teenaged schoolgirls, Pauline Parker and Juliet Hulme, were accused of murdering Parker's mother, whose battered and blood-stained body had been found at Victoria Park on 22 June. The murder made sensational headlines and shocked Christchurch's elite, for Hulme's father was the Rector of Canterbury University College. That such a horrific murder could occur in staid, conservative Christchurch came as a shock to many people, and upset complacent assumptions that 'such things cannot happen here'. Both girls were convicted. (As Ann Perry, Hulme later had a successful career as a novelist.)

The fifties were years of prosperity for Canterbury farmers, which meant prosperity for Christchurch too. The Korean War sent wool prices soaring to unprecedented heights, and some farmers were heard to quip that if this kept up they would all become millionaires. The city's manufacturing sector expanded rapidly in this decade, absorbing a steady stream of British and Dutch migrants and attracting people from other parts of the South Island to settle in Christchurch. The demand for housing was insatiable, and it was a feature of this period that young families often spent a year or so in transit-camp accommodation while waiting for a house. Many people still rode bikes to work or school,

W. A. (Bill) Sutton (1917–), Canterbury's most representative and influential painter since the Second World War. Lectured at the School of Fine Arts, Canterbury University, 1949–79. Christchurch's leading portraitist, he has also created distinctive images of Canterbury's landscape and skies.

Christchurch Star

The Dainty Inn, High Street, 1959. This was one of several American-style milk-bars that were popular places for teenagers to meet on Friday and Saturday nights. Early motorcycle gangs were known as 'milk-bar cowboys'.

Standish and Preece photograph, CM

124

Jazz concert in the Civic Theatre, 19 September 1955, sponsored by Drages' Record Bar. But the rock and roll era was just dawning, and bands such as Max Merritt and the Meteors became the crowd-pullers of the new generation.

J. W. Malloch photograph, CHAC/CM 116/18

but the days of the electric trams and trolley buses were numbered because diesel buses were so much cheaper to run. The last trams departed from the city in September 1954, and the last trolley bus in 1956. But many of the tram-tracks stayed in place for years to come, gradually disappearing under layers of tarseal. More and more people used cars, as soon as they could afford them, and the city's first parking meters appeared in May 1955. The cars were nearly all of British manufacture: Austins, Wolseleys, Hillmans and Vauxhalls. The Morris Minor was easily the most popular car seen on Christchurch streets in this period.

Several notable additions to the city's infrastructure were completed in the late fifties. The conversion of what had previously been a stock route beside the railway into a four-lane expressway was completed with the opening of Blenheim Road in 1957. Designed to relieve congestion in Riccarton Road, it ended in an overbridge beside the Addington Saleyards because public protest had prevented the planners from continuing it across Hagley Park to join St Asaph Street. The park was now sacred turf in a city beset by traffic problems and air pollution. Another arterial road completed in 1959 was Memorial Avenue, linking the city to the airport. This was dedicated as a memorial to airmen killed in the Second World War. The Museum's centennial extensions were finally opened in 1958, and in August 1959 the new Princess Margaret Hospital and nurses' home were opened at the foot of Cashmere Hill. Linwood High School, opened in 1954, was the first of a new design for state secondary schools that became the norm

National Airways Corporation engineering staff, with Vickers Viscount airliner *City of Christchurch*, c. 1958. Harewood now became known as Christchurch International Airport, and embarked on a phase of major development in readiness for the jet age in passenger transport. This aircraft still exists as a static display.

V. C. Browne photograph, CHAC/CM 464

throughout New Zealand over the next two decades, as the 'baby-boom' generation approached secondary-school age. Christchurch's population had grown steadily across this period, from an estimated 135,000 in 1939 to 200,000 in 1959 – a 48 per cent increase, with most of the growth occurring in the forties.

By 1960 the city was beginning to emerge from the drab uniformity of the post-war decade, with signs of growth visible on all sides: new schools, new housing, new roads, more cars and buses, new swimming pools, and even some adventurous new architecture. Christchurch was clearly expanding, with new suburbs being laid out, especially to the north-west. A new phase in the life of the city was about to dawn, in which some of the old certainties and assumptions faded. It was remarkable how quickly the early fifties' mood of reverence for church, monarchy and the Canterbury Pilgrims disappeared in the sixties. Here was a new and younger generation, with different interests and priorities.

Burnside Road was upgraded to a four-lane highway and renamed Memorial Avenue in tribute to airmen killed in the Second World War. It is now the city's gateway from the airport. This photo was taken on 24 August 1959. Burnside Park is on the right, Kendall Avenue at left.

George Weigel photograph, CHAC/CM 1048

CHAPTER SEVEN

Suburban City
1960 – 1979

In contrast to the conformist conservative fifties, Christchurch over the next twenty years rode a roller-coaster of rapid change and controversy which bewildered the elderly and excited the young. These were the years of pop music and protest, 'pot' smoking and the Pill, the Progressive Youth Movement and 'the road through the park'; the Wahine storm, the Vietnam War, the new Town Hall and the Tenth Commonwealth Games. These were the years of Manning, Guthrey, Pickering and Hay as mayors, and of Holyoake, Kirk, Marshall and Muldoon in national politics. The University of Canterbury celebrated its centennial, and Radio Avon took to the air.

In twenty years the city had ten official visits from members of the British royal family, including four by the Queen and the Duke of Edinburgh, but the crowds were never as great as those of 1954. The 1964 visit of the British pop

First of the steel-and-glass boxes that have completely changed the character of Cathedral Square: the Government Life building (1964). At right is the Citizens' War Memorial (1937), Trethewey's masterpiece, and beyond it the classical tower of the old Crystal Palace has been encased in a plain metal box for the Carlton cinema.

Stan McKay photograph, CM

127

group the Beatles drew far bigger crowds of young people than any of the royal tours. Above all, these were the first decades of television, which brought a flood of American entertainment into the living rooms of the city, causing cinemas to close and spending patterns to change. Steam trains disappeared and jumbo jets arrived. The era of suburban shopping malls dawned, and retailers began to desert the inner city. Motorcars proliferated, spawning motels, carpark buildings, overbridges and the one-way street system. High-rise buildings invaded the inner city, causing more change to the townscape in twenty years than in the previous fifty, while the suburbs just kept on sprawling. It was little wonder that the smog got worse and worse.

Christchurch stopped growing in the late seventies and suffered an exodus of population, especially younger adults, to Australia or the North Island. The full employment and prosperity of the early sixties suddenly ended in a sharp recession in 1967, compounded by the oil crisis of 1973 and Britain's entry to the European Economic Community, which curtailed New Zealand's largest traditional export market. New Zealand's terms of trade fell forty per cent in little more than a year. Wool prices dropped, and though alternative markets were

High Street from the Bank of New Zealand building, c. 1960. Fisher's Building (1880) is in the left foreground. The triangle garden (right foreground) marks the site of Cabstand Corner (see page 46).

Stan McKay photograph, CM 13647

Above: Redgrave Street, Halswell, October 1970: typical of new suburban housing developments in Christchurch in the sixties and seventies, with curving streets and underground wiring. These are state houses, which now look much the same as most other developments.

Christchurch Star

Below: A typical petrol station of the sixties: the Ace Service Station, Sydenham, on the corner of Hastings and Colombo Streets. Port Hills in the background.

Stan McKay photograph, CM

An example of the tavern-style bars of the late sixties aimed at changing drinking habits after the abolition of six o'clock closing, with carpets and food.
Stan McKay photograph, CM

found, high inflation and high unemployment dogged the rest of the seventies, only to be worsened by the second oil crisis, of 1979. It was a bit like the 1880s depression all over again, with many people moving to Australia in search of jobs.

At the same time, people lower down the socio-economic ladder moved to Christchurch for similar reasons. The seventies saw a significant influx of Maori and Polynesian migrants, who settled mostly in the eastern suburbs of Christchurch. Some of the Maori had Ngai Tahu connections, but the largest group were Ngati Porou, from the East Coast of the North Island. The city's ethnic profile was starting to change. In 1926 the census found only 144 Maori living in Christchurch; by 1981 there were 4,032 Maori and 7,800 of Maori descent, together comprising 7.2 per cent of the city's population.

Christchurch had grown remarkably in extent during the fifties and sixties. New streets and houses had taken over large areas of farmland in the north-east and north-west, while many vacant blocks across the southern suburbs were now built over. New Brighton was now physically joined to the city by a continuous built-up area, while Hornby and Halswell grew from almost nothing to become satellite dormitory suburbs. Much of the new development to the west took place outside the City Council's boundaries, in Paparua and Waimairi Counties or in Riccarton Borough, and this period saw many wrangles between these local authorities and the city over a variety of issues.

Developers were required to provide ample spaces for parks and sportsgrounds to relieve the tedium of densely packed housing, and Christchurch remains the most generously endowed of all New Zealand cities in its provision of such

Opposite top: The Aulsebrook's factory, corner of Montreal and St Asaph Streets (now part of the one-way system), at its fullest extent in the 1970s. The building was demolished in 1985.
Christchurch Star

Bottom: Foundations being laid for Riccarton Mall, early 1960s. Riccarton Road in foreground, view from north. No houses now remain on this block; the site has been taken over by a greatly expanded mall and carpark, the latter having closed part of Division Street (left).
Stan McKay photograph, CM

131

Massed school choirs performing at the first Pan Pacific Arts Festival, 3 March 1965. Also appearing at this festival were Inia Te Wiata and the conductor Sir Malcolm Sargent.

Christchurch Star

Sir Eruera Tirikatene (1895–1967), Ngai Tahu leader and MP for Southern Maori, 1932–67. A sergeant in the Maori (Pioneer) Battalion in the First World War, he then became a farmer and marine engineer, and a leader in the Ratana Church. He was the first Ratana MP, supporting Labour, and served in the War Cabinet, 1943–45. Knighted in 1960. His daughter Whetu Tirikatene-Sullivan succeeded him as MP for Southern Maori.

Christchurch Star

spaces. Curved streets were preferred, to break the monotonous grid pattern of the old city, and shopping centres were placed at strategic intervals. Bishopdale is a good example of the planned shopping centre also intended to become a community centre, with shops, banks, library and post office grouped around a pedestrian precinct flanked by large carparks. The rapid growth of supermarkets sounded the death-knell for corner dairies and old-style neighbourhood grocery stores, which often fell empty before being demolished.

New suburbs needed more than new shops, however. Schools were the next essential, as the 'baby-boom' generation began to marry and reproduce itself. Christchurch had its biggest-ever school-building boom in this period, with a rash of new primary and intermediate schools funnelling pupils into the new standard-design high schools scattered around the city's periphery. By 1977 Burnside had become the country's biggest high school, with over two thousand pupils on its roll. Christchurch has always had a slightly better-educated population than other New Zealand cities, measured in terms of school and tertiary qualifications. It now became a mecca for ambitious parents because it offered such a wide range of choice in education for their children.

After a century in the heart of the city, the University of Canterbury finally completed its move to the north-west suburb of Ilam in 1975. The site had been acquired in 1949, initially to relocate the School of Engineering, but as student numbers grew steadily across the 1950s, then rapidly across the 1960s, the removal of the whole University became unavoidable. The School of Fine Arts joined the engineers in temporary accommodation at Ilam in the early sixties, while a major building programme transformed the block between Ilam and Clyde Roads. The Christchurch Teachers' College also moved out to Ilam in the seventies, the secondary division in 1970 and the rest of the college in 1978. After housing part of the Christchurch Technical Institute for a few years, the old University buildings on the 'Town Site' were finally taken over by a trust

132

board in 1978 to become the Arts Centre of Christchurch, now a highly successful tourist attraction on the Worcester Boulevard.

Christchurch manufacturing in 1972 employed over 36,000 people in 1,210 factories, both figures about 15 per cent of their New Zealand totals. Industrial production was worth $470 million, about 12 per cent of the New Zealand total. Christchurch employed just over half of the country's rubber workers, and accounted for 43 per cent of its rubber goods. Since 1960, while the number of food and beverage factories had declined slightly, those involved in metal products, transport equipment, machinery and electrical appliances had all increased substantially. Half of Christchurch's factories were still in the inner city, but nearly all of the new jobs in manufacturing between 1959 and 1969 were in the suburban industrial zones of Hornby, Papanui, Bromley and Woolston, and this trend continued through the seventies. Many inner-city blocks on either side of Moorhouse Avenue (and in Waltham and Phillipstown) were cleared of old wooden houses in this period and replaced by steel-framed all-purpose warehouses, which could be used as stores or small factories. Many of the new firms occupying these premises were relatively small, employing only a dozen or twenty workers, and some went under in the 1973 recession, but they made the city's inner industrial zone a busy and bustling place.

By 1975 the University of Canterbury had completed its move from the old Town Site to the suburb of Ilam, where the School of Engineering (foreground) and the School of Fine Arts had led the move more than a decade earlier.

Frank McGregor photograph, CM

133

Christchurch has been home to a number of notable inventions. Probably its most famous is the Hamilton jet boat, invented by a South Canterbury run-holder, C. W. F. (later Sir William) Hamilton. He was also an engineer and developed his idea in a small factory in Annex Road. His first commercial units were marketed in 1957, and the factory grew rapidly to meet strong international demand across the sixties and seventies. Jet boats are now widely used around the world and are especially useful in shallow waters. But the idea of a high-pressure water pump to power a small boat only became a commercial possibility with the development of fibreglass hulls, another technology that Christchurch helped pioneer.

In the 1950s most people got to and from work on bikes or trams; in the 1960s they wanted to drive their own cars. The streets became clogged with traffic at the rush hours, and the city consulted overseas experts to help find solutions for the future. Detailed surveys of traffic flows and projected growth zones provided the basis for a master transportation plan, unveiled in 1962. Two major motorways were envisaged heading into the city from the north and the south-west. These were intended to join expressways which in time would form a ring road, moving traffic rapidly around the outer suburbs. The inner city was to be served by pairs of one-way streets with computer-controlled lights, creating 'green waves' of advancing traffic, while the conversion of several streets to pedestrian malls would be served by strategically placed carpark buildings.

Papanui in the early 1970s: St Paul's, centre foreground. Intersection of Papanui, Harewood and Main North Roads, lower right. Northlands Shopping Mall centre, Papanui High School centre left.

Christchurch Star

Such was the plan, and most of its major elements were in place and operating by the end of the seventies. However, some parts were never built. The northern motorway from Belfast to Kaiapoi was completed by 1967, but strong opposition from St Albans residents blocked construction of the final corridor from Belfast to the inner city. The first stage of the Brougham Street expressway cut a swathe across the southern part of the city, though its proposed motorway link to bypass Hornby never eventuated. Ironically, the city at last got a new railway station in 1960, just before the steam era ended (1971) and passenger transport by rail began a steep decline.

Elsie Locke (1912–) prolific writer, mainly for children, and tenacious campaigner for peace and environment. Helped edit *Women Today,* 1937–39, and was a key figure in Campaign for Nuclear Disarmament, 1957–70. *The Runaway Settlers* (1965) was the first of several books with historical Canterbury settings. Bicultural theme prominent in *Maori King and British Queen* (1974), *The Kauri and the Willow* (1984), and *Two Peoples, One Land* (1988). Awarded Hon.Litt.D. by the University of Canterbury in 1987.

Christchurch Star

Brougham Street expressway, 1978, looking west across Lincoln Road, with earthworks for two flyovers taking shape. Motorway developments usually meant the demolition or removal of many older houses.

Christchurch Star

135

Right: Road tunnel to Lyttelton nearing completion. Opened on 27 February 1962, it was designed as a toll tunnel (New Zealand's longest) but soon paid for itself and became toll-free in 1979.

Christchurch Star

Below: Lyttelton on the eve of the container revolution. Cashin Quay, at top, opened in November 1964. The first container crane started work here in June 1977.

CM 16270

After decades of planning and debate, Christchurch at last had direct road access to its port in 1964. When the Lyttelton road tunnel opened, tolls were charged and its staff wore American-style uniforms, but greater-than-expected traffic flows soon repaid the government's investment and the tunnel became toll-free (with far fewer staff) in 1979. A new expressway linked the tunnel to Ferry Road, but most of the heavy traffic soon preferred the short cut through Opawa to join the end of the Brougham Street expressway, creating serious problems of noise and congestion for residents of Opawa and Port Hills Road. A new road/rail freight terminal was built in Waltham in 1970 to ease overloading at the old railway goods sheds.

Most of the heavy traffic came from the new container facility at the port. Containers revolutionised sea transport in the seventies and soon made the old wharf cranes at Lyttelton redundant. The new container facility was built on reclaimed land east of Gladstone Pier and named Cashin Quay; it was opened in 1964. A far greater tonnage of cargo now left Lyttelton in containers, and came to the port on road transport, than had previously been carried by rail and handled by the wharfies. These major changes in transport technology affected Lyttelton greatly, and in a very short space of time. Regular daily passenger services by rail came to an end as fewer and fewer wharfies needed to travel to

New Railway Station, Moorhouse Avenue, 1960. Designed in the thirties but delayed by the war, this well-proportioned brick building was obsolete within a decade, as passengers deserted the railways for motor cars and air travel. It now houses Science Alive and a cinema complex.

Christchurch Star

137

the port. The electric trains were withdrawn and the overhead wires dismantled. Lyttelton became a quiet backwater, with deserted wharves and empty houses, as giant container ships could be loaded in hours rather than days by a mere handful of men.

Christchurch Airport grew as rapidly as Lyttelton declined. More and more people preferred air travel, especially as the Viscounts and Friendships were replaced by Boeing 737 jets after 1968. Paul Pascoe designed the new airport terminal, which was opened in 1960, to cope with the coming jet age in civil aviation. The opening of the new runways was marked in March 1964 with an Air Expo, which also celebrated the fiftieth anniversary of the first flight between Christchurch and Timaru. Operation Deep Freeze continued to use Christchurch as its gateway to Antarctica, and in 1974 the world's biggest transport plane, a Lockheed Galaxy, visited the airport for the first time. Regular jet services to Australia had commenced with DC-8 aircraft in 1965, and in 1972 the first Boeing 747 jumbo jet airliner landed at Christchurch. The domestic terminal was almost doubled in size in 1975, and the first stage of a new international terminal was opened in December 1979.

While new expressways and overbridges were highly visible changes to the city's infrastructure, no less important for the health of the population were major developments in drainage and sewerage. Construction of a new sewage-treatment plant at Bromley was completed in 1962 at a cost of £1.3 million. This gave the necessary capacity to complete the reticulation of sewers to all parts of the metropolitan area, especially the new north-west suburbs. But the treatment works soon became overloaded, and in the late sixties nearby residents complained about the bad odours emanating from the works. The 'Aranui

Smog was a perennial winter problem for Christchurch throughout this period and beyond. The city's worst daytime smog level was recorded in June 1977, but night-time levels were usually a great deal worse.

Christchurch Star

Left: The new passenger terminal and control tower, Christchurch Airport, under construction alongside the old control tower. Designed by Paul Pascoe, this award-winning building still serves the purpose for which it was built.

V. C. Browne photograph, CM

Below: Christchurch International Airport, 1965. Wartime barracks (left) have been largely taken over by the US Navy for its Deepfreeze Operation personnel. NAC hangers and engineering facilities upper left, Airwork and aero club hangars at right. White Heron Hotel (now Airport Plaza) under construction in foreground.

CM 16271

smell' became a big issue for the eastern side of Christchurch, climaxing in 1973 when the Drainage Board brought in American consultants to solve the problem. They advised changes in the biological treatment process, to relieve the load on the oxidation ponds, and two new trickling-filter towers were built in 1976 and 1978. But the smell recurred in hot weather, and the towers were covered with huge fibreglass domes in 1986–87, forming the city's most visible landmarks from the air.

While improved drainage dealt with the worst effects of wet southerly storms, Christchurch still had to cope with its old curse, the hot nor'wester. In February 1973 the city baked in a record 41.6°C temperature with strong winds. Poultry farmers lost over twenty thousand birds in the heat, and a grass fire on Clifton Hill near Sumner destroyed five houses. Later that day, a south-west change lowered the temperature by a record 28°. The nor'wester battered the city again in August 1975, when a severe gale with wind gusts up to 172 kph caused serious damage and over two hundred minor injuries in Canterbury. But these were the only major threats from nature in this period, apart from the Wahine storm of 1968. The Waimakariri River was behaving itself within well-maintained stopbanks.

This period was a boom time for Ryan Brothers, the city's leading demolition contractors. Every week, it seemed, old brick buildings in the inner city were reduced to piles of rubble and replaced with plain boxes of glass and steel. For older citizens, this was a profoundly unsettling period as they saw their familiar landmarks transformed, and not always for the better. Cathedral Square suffered the most radical transformation, as its well-proportioned Edwardian buildings were replaced by an assortment of high-rise boxes completely at odds with the scale of the cathedral. The first of the newcomers was the Government Life building, which displayed time and temperature in lights from its rooftop. The old Bank of New Zealand building was supposed to be incorporated in a new development, but it was almost casually swept away in 1967. The old Dalgety's and Tramway Board offices disappeared in 1970, to be replaced by the even taller slabs of Carruca House and the Housing Corporation. On the opposite side of the Square, the new CML and AMP buildings were completed in 1975, the latter connected by a carpark to Noahs Hotel, on the site of the old Gas Company offices. All this rebuilding was accompanied by changes to the traffic flows, designed to make the Square a friendlier place for pedestrians. The roadway in front of the cathedral was closed in 1965, and that in front of the Post Office in 1972. But the Square remained the hub of the city's public transport network, and was always full of red buses in the rush hour.

The most important new building project for the city as a whole in this period was undoubtedly the new Town Hall complex. There had been many past proposals for a new town hall, but the Depression and the Second World War had shelved all these plans, and a new initiative was needed after the war. The driving force behind the Christchurch Town Hall project was Sir James Hay, founder of Hay's department store. The site chosen was that of the old Limes Hospital on Kilmore Street, overlooking the Avon River and Victoria Square. A large auditorium for concerts was linked to a theatre and large reception areas. Sir James Hay did not live to see this great project completed, but the theatre was named after him in recognition of his key role. Opened in September 1972, the new Town Hall was acclaimed as an architectural gem and the best civic amenity of its kind in the country. The Ferrier fountain, donated by a local businessman, added a distinctive finishing touch to a fine group of buildings.

The mayors of this period were two of the city's most popular and two of its most controversial. Sir George Manning (1958–68) was a Labour mayor who led Citizens-dominated councils in 1959, 1962 and 1965 (the 1959 council had no Labour councillors at all). Yet he was enormously popular, an efficient and impartial chairman, and a genial civic leader. At his retirement in 1968, he had completed thirty-four years of service on the City Council. His successor was Ron Guthrey (1968–71), founder of a highly successful carrying firm. He had been a driving force behind the rapid expansion of Christchurch Airport, in collaboration with its general manager, Ivan Jamieson. Guthrey declared that he wanted to be an administrative mayor rather than just a social figurehead, and he galvanised the City Council on many fronts, pushing ahead long-overdue projects. He put his full weight behind Ron Scott's efforts to make Christchurch the venue for the Tenth Commonwealth Games, scheduled for 1974, and fully supported the implementation of the city's master transportation plan. The latter proved his undoing.

Christchurch Town Hall (1972) and the Ferrier fountain, viewed across the Avon from Victoria Square. Designed by Warren and Mahoney, this award-winning group of buildings has become a New Zealand classic.
CM 16276

141

Richard Tayler winning the 10,000 metres event at the Tenth Commonwealth Games, Christchurch, 1974. This was the first live colour TV coverage of a major sporting event in New Zealand.
Christchurch Star

Opposite: Show Day, 1965: the Grand Parade in progress at the Addington Show Grounds. Canterbury Court exhibition hall (built in the early sixties) centre left, livestock sheds upper right. The rest of the site is crowded with sideshows and agricultural machinery. Canterbury Court survives, but nearly all the other buildings have gone since the A&P Association moved to new premises near Wigram.
V. C. Browne photo, CM

Part of this plan called for the realignment of Harper Avenue across North Hagley Park to join the one-way system at Salisbury Street, but there was strong public opposition to this proposal, and legal action delayed the work through 1971. Guthrey had already become a controversial mayor for removing a wreath placed on the War Memorial by the Progressive Youth Movement on Anzac Day in 1970. He had clashed with the chairman of Waimairi County, Barry Rich, over the city's purchase of Mona Vale in 1968, and over many other issues. As the local body election of 1971 approached, the City Council decided on Porritt Park and the Centennial Pool as the main Games venues, but Neville Pickering (the Labour candidate) favoured Queen Elizabeth II Park (the former New Brighton trotting course, renamed in 1963), and campaigned successfully on this and the 'road through the park' issue in a lively and acrimonious election. Guthrey was narrowly defeated, and Pickering's predominantly Labour council quickly confirmed the New Brighton venue for the Games, despite predictions of escalating costs.

Months of meticulous planning by local committees and sports groups made the Tenth Commonwealth Games of 1974 one of the most successful ever held. The whole city seemed to get involved, and the warm welcome shown to visiting athletes led them to call this the friendliest games ever. Live international television coverage gave the city unprecedented publicity overseas, and helped establish Christchurch as a major New Zealand tourist destination.

This was a great period for sport and the outdoors in Christchurch. Thousands took up jogging, no doubt inspired by the Games, and in March 1975 some three thousand people took part in the first 'City to Surf' fun-run. Hagley Park became a favourite track for lunch-hour joggers, but in the winter months they complained that the air was not fit to breathe. Record smog levels were recorded in June 1975, far in excess of World Health Organisation guidelines, and in 1977 the city's worst-ever daytime smog levels were recorded. The Clean Air Society campaigned long and hard to remedy the city's major environmental health problem, and had some success in getting domestic clean-air zones introduced, but the problem persists, largely because Christchurch's location makes it prone to temperature-inversion layers in frosty weather, which trap smoke and fumes near the ground.

Musically this was a period of great activity and expansion in popular entertainment, and a period of great controversy in traditional circles. Rock and roll reached New Zealand in the fifties, radically changing music and dance styles among teenagers. Local bands sprang up in imitation of American and British groups. The influence of the Beatles and their many rivals and imitators was pervasive, reinforced by radio and television. CHTV3 began transmission in 1961, but radio was the greater medium for pop music (and advertising) for most of the sixties, and Radio Avon was launched in 1973 to cater for a largely local listening audience. Pop music and the contraceptive pill changed the lifestyle of Christchurch teenagers in the sixties more completely than in any previous generation, much to the dismay of many middle-aged and elderly citizens who complained about a collapse of moral standards.

The city's traditional music circles were deeply disrupted in the seventies by a bitter dispute known as the 'two-orchestra crisis', in which the Civic Orchestra (renamed Christchurch Symphony Orchestra in 1974) became the victim of

a complicated factional struggle and a clash of personalities, principles and politics, which spilled over into the media and took up time in City Council meetings. The rest of the city looked on with amazement at one of Christchurch's most spectacular civic controversies.

In the meantime, however, Christchurch could claim to be regarded as the country's leading centre in the dramatic arts, with Ngaio Marsh's last Shakespearean productions for the University's drama society in the sixties, and flourishing amateur companies such as the Repertory Society attracting good audiences. In retrospect, the founding of the Court Theatre in 1971 was a landmark. This was the city's first professional theatre company, and the fact that it has survived and prospered to the present day, launching the careers of numerous New Zealand actors, designers and musicians, speaks volumes for the city's cultural awareness and Elric Hooper's leadership.

Neville Pickering lasted only one term as mayor. He was defeated by Hamish Hay (son of Sir James Hay), who went on to become Christchurch's longest-serving mayor (1974–89). Anxious to dampen the political polarities that had emerged under Guthrey and Pickering, Hay set out to be a non-political mayor who had the interests of the city as a whole at heart. At forty-six he was the city's youngest mayor since Bob Macfarlane in 1938, and soon proved himself to be a most conscientious and diplomatic mayor. In 1975 Vicki Buck, at nineteen, became New Zealand's youngest-ever city councillor, at the start of an outstanding career in local government.

Sir Hamish Hay (1927–), Christchurch's longest-serving mayor, 1974–89. Born in Christchurch, educated at St Andrew's College and Canterbury University College, he was first elected to the city council in 1959. Knighted in 1982, he has chaired many public boards and trusts, including the Christchurch Town Hall, Canterbury Museum, Canterbury United Council and Museum of New Zealand.

Christchurch Star

Cathedral Square, 30 April 1971, when over six thousand protesters marched against New Zealand's involvement in the Vietnam War.

Christchurch Star

144

Although Canterbury's share of New Zealand's population had fallen to 13 per cent by 1976, the province still regarded itself as a force to be reckoned with in national politics. Christchurch's electoral boundaries changed significantly in this period, yet it remained a Labour stronghold, and the home of the leader of the Labour Party from 1965, the former Kaiapoi mayor, Norman Kirk. He became Prime Minister in November 1972, heading the Third Labour Government, which then faced one of the country's sharpest economic recessions. His independent stance in foreign policy, opposing French nuclear testing in the South Pacific, struck a chord with many Christchurch voters. Kirk was at the height of his powers and popularity when he died unexpectedly in August 1974. His successor, Bill Rowling, who also had strong links with Christchurch, was defeated in the 1975 general election by National's Rob Muldoon. Christchurch (and the South Island) were to have far less clout in national politics during the Muldoon years (1975–84).

At the end of the seventies Christchurch faced an uncertain future. Economic recession was bankrupting smaller businesses, and in 1980 there were 10,725 Christchurch people registered as unemployed or on relief work, about ten per cent of the adult workforce. This was the city's worst unemployment figure since the Depression of the thirties. Inflation had made the dollar worth only a third of its 1970 value, and many low-income families struggled to survive. Christchurch now had more visible contrasts between rich and poor than it had known for several generations. The wealthy elite of old families, successful industrialists and businessmen had been joined by newly rich property developers and entrepreneurs, but at the other end of the scale there were families living in dire poverty in Aranui, Woolston or Addington. In between, the middle classes found that inflation had pushed them into higher tax brackets, just when the mass media was urging them to spend more on cars and consumer goods. Concern for law and order increased as crime rates grew and motorcycle gangs terrorised their neighbours and each other. No wonder that so many Christchurch people turned to sport, gambling, beer and television for solace in this period.

Norman Kirk (1923–74), Prime Minister of New Zealand, 1972–74. A former engine driver with only primary-school education, he was the country's youngest mayor (of Kaiapoi) in 1953. MP for Lyttelton from 1957, then for Sydenham, he became leader of the Labour Party in 1965 and achieved remarkable stature as Prime Minister. A commanding orator with great warmth and compassion, Kirk might have become a second Seddon but for his untimely death.

Christchurch Star

CHAPTER EIGHT

Regional Metropolis

1980 – 1999

Ian Brackenbury Channell (1932–), 'The Wizard of New Zealand'. Claims to be a 'living work of art' but refuses to be counted by the census. He was closely involved with Alf's Imperial Army and became famous for repainting Telecom's new blue telephone boxes red. His lunchtime lectures in Cathedral Square and other exploits have irritated or delighted thousands. It is now hard to imagine the city without his unpredictable presence.

Christchurch Star

However unsettling the seventies had been, the eighties were to be 'something else again', as American tourists were apt to remark of Christchurch itself. Change had become a way of life, at an even faster pace. For the country as a whole, this was the decade of the fourth Labour government and 'Rogernomics', when New Zealand became once again a social laboratory for the world, reversing the over-regulated welfare state set in place by the first Labour government of the thirties. Free-market reforms decentralised government and the economy, causing the biggest structural changes New Zealand had seen in half a century.

In Christchurch these were the years of anti-Springbok tour protests; of Hamish Hay as mayor; of the Wizard, the Bird Man and the Bible Lady as 'characters' of Cathedral Square; of more royal tours and a visit by the Pope; of the City Mall and Metro refuse stations; the closure of the gasworks, railway station and Addington railway workshops; the rebuilding of Christchurch Hospital and the Polytechnic; the advent of the Tranz-Alpine tourist train and yet more high-rise towers in the central city; of Orana Park and Meadowbank; the Halswell tornado and the big snow of '92; of Lotto and Sunday trading; of Geoffrey Palmer and Mike Moore as successive Prime Ministers just before National swept back into power in 1990.

Local-government reform in 1989 at last made Christchurch in name what it had long been in fact, a true regional metropolis. Amalgamation ended the anomalous situation of Riccarton Borough and two county councils administering large suburban areas on the city's western flank. Christchurch City Council now administered a coherent urban area, while the Canterbury Regional Council administered the rural hinterland. The City Council's move to new civic offices in the former Miller's Building in Tuam Street coincided with these changes and became symbolic of them. The city's population in 1991 was 289,077, after low growth rates of only about 2.4 per cent through the eighties. But in the next six years the city reached 320,500. This was an increase of 10.8 per cent: not far behind Auckland's growth rate in the same period and well above Wellington's. Christchurch was now New Zealand's second-largest territorial local authority, second only to Auckland City. It had long been the largest urban centre in the South Island; it now housed a third of the South Island's population, and nearly three-quarters of the people living in Canterbury.

Migration was the driving force behind Christchurch's growth in the nineties. This was the decade of the so-called 'Asian invasion', which transformed Avonhead to such an extent that taxi drivers made jokes about going to 'Asianhead'. Most of the new migrants came from Malaysia, Taiwan, Japan and Korea, with smaller numbers from Hong Kong and China. They brought with them substantial sums for investment, and often impressive qualifications and entrepreneurial skills. Unlike most of history's migrants, who start their new life at the bottom of the heap, Christchurch's Asian migrants drove expensive cars and set up new businesses, sending their children to private schools and then to Canterbury or Lincoln University.

Even so, there were substantial movements of non-Asians both in and out of Christchurch in the nineties. Several thousand left to live in Australia, while nearly 35,000 people left Christchurch to live elsewhere in New Zealand; but these were balanced by nearly 38,000 who came to see what life was like in the Garden City. By 1996 over eighty per cent of the city's residents were New

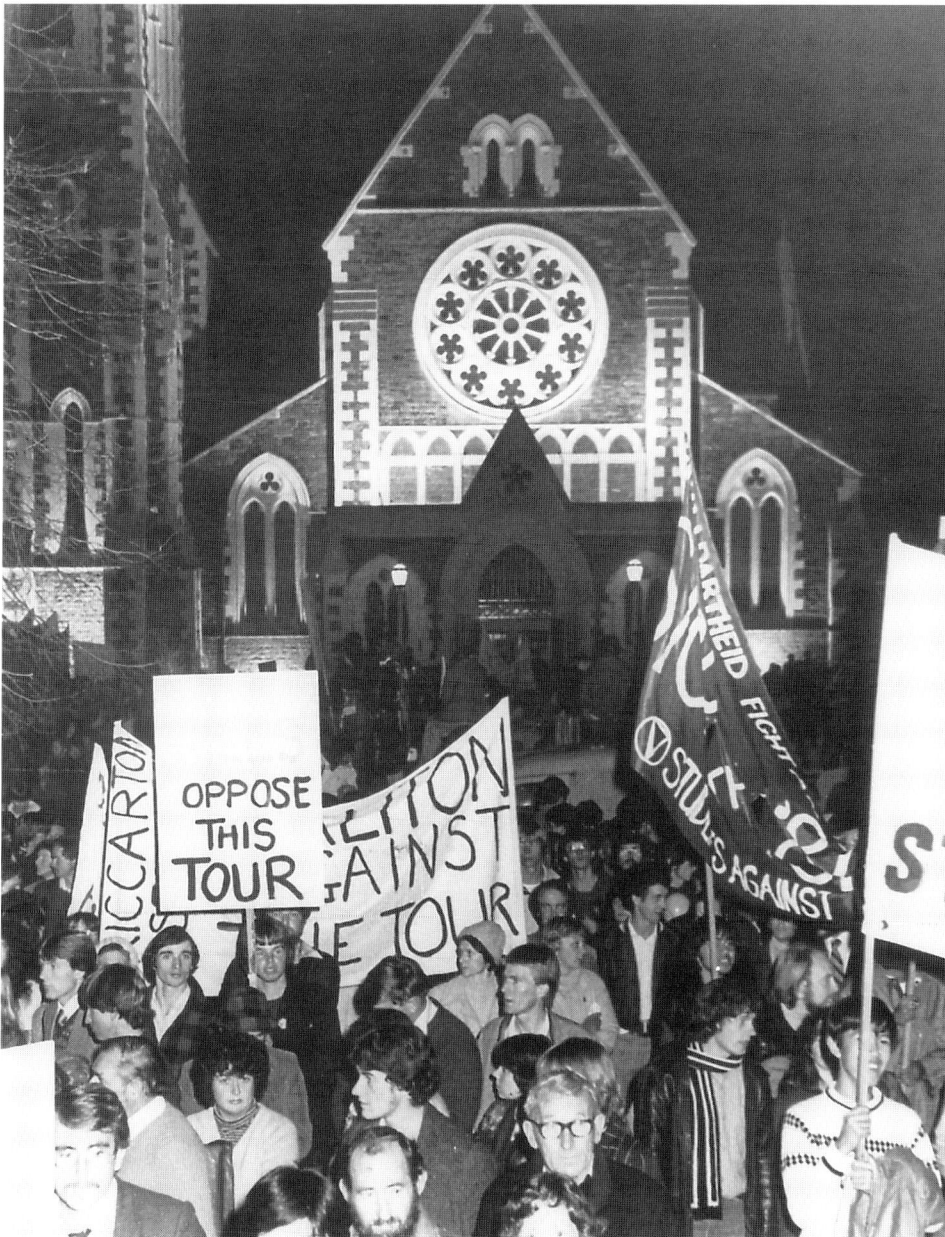

Crowds in Cathedral Square protest against the Springbok rugby tour of 1981. The government's decision to let this tour proceed polarised the country and brought middle-class New Zealanders opposed to the apartheid regime in South Africa onto the streets.

Christchurch Star

147

Vicki Buck (1955–), Mayor of Christchurch, 1989–98. Elected to the City Council in 1975 at age nineteen, she was educated at New Brighton Primary, Christchurch Girls' High School and Canterbury University (MA in Political Science, 1976). Must rank as one of the city's most popular and effective civic leaders.

Christchurch Star

Zealand-born Europeans. Just under seven per cent were Maori, compared with fourteen per cent nationally. The largest non-New Zealand-born group came from Britain, significantly more than in the rest of the country. Although highly visible, Asians comprised only four per cent of the city's population in 1996, and were slightly fewer in number than residents who hailed from Canada, the USA, Europe and South Africa combined.

The nineties in Christchurch are inseparable from the mayoralty of Vicki Buck (1989–98), Christchurch's youngest and first woman mayor. Here was a dynamic and positive civic leader, whose broad smile and infectious laugh conveyed the message that life was to be enjoyed and that Christchurch was a great place in which to enjoy it. A new city logo was adopted in the nineties, showing the Cathedral spire against a blue sky with a stream winding through green fields. Two slogans were offered: 'The Garden City', and 'The City that Shines', neatly combining the traditional view with Vicki Buck's progressivist image – and Christchurch's chronic failure to agree on any one thing! Her encouragement of bright ideas from council staff made the city buzz with a new sense of purpose in these years. Profits from the council-owned electricity supplier Southpower kept rates at a reasonable level and financed a range of major civic-enhancement projects.

The council now sponsored summertime concerts in Hagley Park, catering for fans of jazz, rock and country music, climaxing with classical music and fireworks in the late summer. Christchurch's streets were full of Japanese cars, as importers flooded the market with near-new second-hand imports. This decade also saw a redesigned Victoria Square, the Parkroyal Hotel, Worcester Boulevard and the return of vintage electric trams to the inner city. Airport buildings kept having to be extended or rebuilt to cope with increasing use as tourism became part of the city's economic lifeblood. Even the Cathedral acquired a controversial new visitors' centre to cope with the influx of tourists.

Fisher's Building in 1985, cleaned and spruced up but now overshadowed by the National Mutual and Reserve Bank buildings on Hereford Street. Cycling has made a big comeback with the advent of lighter, faster, ten-speed bikes.

Joan Woodward photograph, CM 7267/10

Above: Cathedral Square in the 1980s, looking east down Worcester Street.

Christchurch Star

Below: Looking towards the Square from the south-east, 1983: the Cathedral spire peeping over the top of the BNZ building. High Street has become a pedestrian mall with an overbridge.

Christchurch Star

New Zealand's first casino opened in Christchurch in 1994, also with tourists in mind. The Mount Cavendish gondola was another controversial tourist project of this period, which has never matched the optimistic forecasts of its promoters, but a great deal of local effort and fund-raising finally gave New Brighton its second pier in 1997, an elegant concrete concourse for fishermen and weekend strollers. The addition of a new public library at the pier's entrance has proved highly successful. This was also the decade of professional rugby, when the Canterbury Crusaders in the Super 12 series aroused as many one-eyed red-and-black supporters and as much local fervour as any Ranfurly Shield game in the fifties. Lancaster Park now has floodlights, whose ugly steel gantries are the tallest structures on the city's eastern side.

Several suburban shopping malls were built or rebuilt in this decade on a grandiose scale, with food halls, multiplex cinemas and yet more shops. Northlands and Riccarton Malls were completely transformed, while on the other side of the city Eastgate and the Palms sprang up, adorned with American fast-food outlets. Traditional corner fish-and-chip shops struggled to compete with McDonald's and Kentucky Fried Chicken, while a whole range of exotic eating establishments — Japanese, Thai, Korean, Indian — followed the wave of Asian migration. In the inner city, changed licensing laws spawned a rash of small bars and restaurants which often placed chairs and tables on the pavement out front, giving Oxford Terrace near Cashel Street a vaguely Parisian appearance. No longer could one just ask for a cup of coffee: would it be latté, cappuccino or espresso? Christchurch's night-life also changed radically, with nightclubs and massage parlours taking over empty commercial premises in the central business district.

A few tall buildings now dominated the inner city. Familiar landmarks such as the old Post Office or the Provincial Council Buildings, and the Cathedral itself, seemed to be submerged in a rising sea of glass and concrete. Despite strong public protests, a vast postal sorting centre was built in Hereford Street in the early eighties, dwarfing the old Public Library. Then a monolithic Telecom Centre rose behind the façade of the old Post Office in Cathedral Square, looking like something out of Noddy's Toytown. An even taller tower rose behind the preserved façade of the Clarendon Hotel, dwarfing Noahs Hotel opposite, not to mention Hurst Seager's original municipal building on the site of the 1850 Land Office, or the Scott statue opposite. The United Service Hotel was demolished in 1990 to make way for a bland bank building, but at least this key corner was spared the indignity of another tower.

Christchurch lost fourteen listed historic buildings in the early nineties. The King Edward Barracks were dismantled and moved to a rural site, leaving a vast carpark awaiting development. In lower Manchester Street, the imposing classical façade of the Kaiapoi Woollen Mills building was lost after engineers declared the rest of the structure unsafe; the site became a car-sale yard. A key cinema in the Square, the Savoy (formerly Liberty), was demolished as the first stage of a redevelopment involving the old Lyttelton Times building, which was then halted by a legal challenge, leaving the site an ugly gap on this side of the Square. While visitors are impressed by the number of heritage buildings Christchurch has saved in comparison with Auckland or Wellington, locals are more likely to lament the losses of recent years.

Sir Richard Hadlee (1951–), New Zealand's most famous cricketer, knighted in 1990, when he held the world record for most wickets (431) in test cricket. The Hadlee Stand at Lancaster Park (now Jade Stadium) recognises the outstanding contribution to Canterbury cricket of Walter Hadlee and his sons.
Christchurch Star

Opposite top: Crowd in Cathedral Square, estimated at seven thousand, in August 1984 for a $2,500 'money drop' publicity stunt by Radio Avon 'to bring some fun and life into a grey Christchurch winter'.
Christchurch Star

Bottom: Soon after the start of the 1987 'City to Surf' fun-run. The Commonwealth Games held in Christchurch in 1974 inspired a whole generation to keep fit by jogging.
Christchurch Star

Above: Cashel Street from the Bridge of Remembrance, 1985, before construction of a mirror-glass office building on this corner. The old brick building with the sagging verandah had been here since the 1860s, and the location was known as Kiddey's Corner, after Walter Edward Kiddey, whose cycle repair and manufacturing shop occupied this building for over half a century. A few doors further along Cashel Street, Fail's Café was for many years the city's best seafood restaurant.

Joan Woodward photograph, CM 7431/2

Below: Victoria Street, looking south-east, 1985. Art Deco design NZR Road Services building at left, soon to be demolished to provide a site for the Casino. Victoria Street has been closed at the Kilmore Street intersection: the Parkroyal Hotel now blocks this view of the Port Hills.

Joan Woodward photograph, CM 7083/11

Demolition of the United Service Hotel, 1990, to make way for the ANZ Bank building between Hereford Street and Cathedral Square.

Christchurch Star

Demolition of the Masonic Lodge in Gloucester Street, 1993, to make way for an apartment block.

Steve Goodenough photograph, CM

Above: Nazareth House, Sydenham, survived the widening of Brougham Street (when it acquired a replica of its old front fence), but this imposing former orphanage and rest home was demolished in 1989.

Joan Woodward photograph, CM 7080/4

Below: The former Kaiapoi Woollen Mills building, Manchester Street, was built about 1912 with an imposing façade designed by the Luttrell brothers. Despite public protest, it was demolished in 1996 to become a car yard.

Christchurch Star

Tourism now grew strongly in Christchurch, with a thirty per cent increase in visitors between 1992 and 1996. The city hosted 602,000 visitors in 1995, with an average stay of 4.2 days. Altogether they spent $388 million, but their economic impact in generating services, employment and consumption was estimated at $931 million. For every dollar spent by a tourist, the local economy was said to benefit by $2.40. The Asian economic downturn drastically reduced the numbers coming from Malaysia and Korea, but the booming economies of North America and Europe made up any shortfall, as the weaker New Zealand dollar made Christchurch an attractive destination despite its remoteness from the rest of the world. Tourist numbers were scarcely affected by the tragedy of October 1995 when a sudden weather change sent a hot-air balloon into the sea off New Brighton, drowning three Japanese tourists.

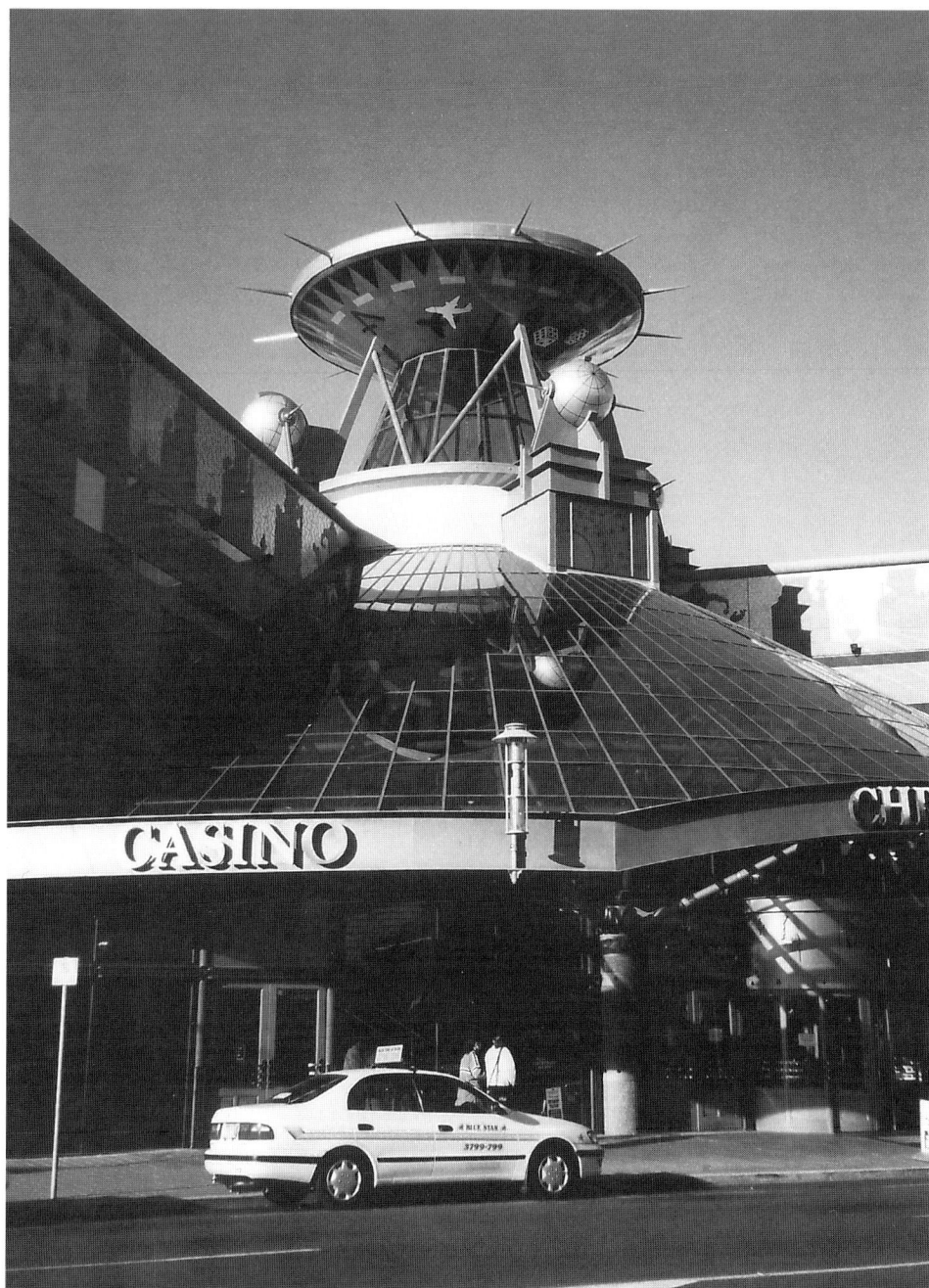

Margaret Mahy (1936–), internationally acclaimed children's writer, with over a hundred published works. Winner of the Carnegie Medal and Esther Glen Medal for children's literature. Extensive work in schools and publications, encouraging children to enjoy reading.
Christchurch Star

Gil Simpson (1948–), company director and chairman of Christchurch City Mission. Educated at Christchurch Boys' High School, co-inventor of computer software system LINC (distributed worldwide by UNISYS) and founder of Aoraki Corporation 1982. New Zealand's most innovative software developer, a major Christchurch employer and export-earner.
Christchurch Star

Christchurch's Casino (1994) was New Zealand's first, designed by Warren and Mahoney to occupy the triangle at the intersection of Victoria and Durham Streets previously occupied by the Road Services depot (see page 152).

New Christchurch Railway Station, Addington (1993), designed by Thom Craig. The 1883 concrete water tower is all that remains of the Addington Railway Workshops (see page 103).

The City Council responded positively to the needs of increased tourism, building a $16 million Convention Centre in Kilmore Street, linked to the Town Hall by a pedestrian overbridge. After taking over Trustbank (which traced its origins to the Canterbury Savings Bank of the sixties), the Australian-owned bank WestpacTrust sponsored a $20 million all-weather stadium beside Addington Raceway. These facilities made Christchurch an attractive option for touring bands and entertainers, as well as major international conferences and sports events, further enhancing its role as a regional metropolis.

The nineties were above all else the decade of electronic gadgetry and the worldwide information revolution made possible by personal computers. Shoppers had to get used to EFTPOS, bank cards and ATMs. Just as microwave ovens had become commonplace in nearly every New Zealand household, so too did cellphones and personal computers in most middle-class homes. (Per capita, New Zealand has one of the world's highest rates of ownership of computers.) Access to e-mail and the Internet dramatically reduced Christchurch's geographic remoteness.

Christchurch became New Zealand's leading centre for computer software, marketing its innovations worldwide. When Lancaster Park sought corporate sponsorship, many citizens were puzzled by its new name, Jade Stadium, and were unaware that this was the brand name of one of the city's most successful overseas exports. Gil Simpson's Aoraki Corporation (founded in 1982) specialised in software such as LINC, which enabled large companies to form networks with their computer systems, and had found ingenious solutions to problems that had baffled the giant multinationals in this field. They now beat a path to his door, making Simpson one of Christchurch's newest millionaires. In 1992 Aoraki's exports were worth $28 million, nearly double New Zealand's wine exports that year.

While Christchurch was showing ingenuity in the field of computer software, one of its young engineers was about to revolutionise the design of racing motorbikes. John Britten was only thirty-eight when he unveiled his radical new design, which made innovative use of carbon fibre. The Britten V1000 motorbike went on to win several major world races in the early nineties, and established four world speed records in 1993. But the inventor then fell ill with cancer and died in 1995. As a symbol of Kiwi ingenuity, the Britten motorbike now has pride of place in Te Papa, the Museum of New Zealand, in Wellington.

Tait Electronics was another Christchurch company that established itself as a major New Zealand exporter in this period. Sir Angus Tait's firm had specialised in the field of radio-telephones, and demonstrated both a high standard of technical excellence and a readiness to explore new technologies and new markets. While PDL remained a major exporter of electrical components and appliances, Sir Robertson Stewart's son Robert soon showed himself to be made of the same stuff by establishing Skope Industries, now one of New Zealand's leading manufacturers of electric heaters. Christchurch's manufacturing sector has not been short of flair or skill in the late twentieth century.

While ever-larger container ships carried away the province's exports from the Cashin Quay container terminal (which now has two container cranes), Lyttelton became a busier port thanks to its use as a base by chartered foreign

Cathedral Square under snow, 29 August 1992. Although not as heavy as previous record snowfalls in 1918 and 1945, this one still gave many people a day at home as transport was disrupted and schools were closed.

Martin Woodhall photograph, *Christchurch Star*

David Caygill (1948–), lawyer, former MP and Cabinet minister. Educated at St Albans Primary, Christchurch Boys' High School and University of Canterbury (BA 1971, LLB 1974). Labour MP for St Albans, 1978–96, Minister of Trade and Industry 1984–88. Minister of Finance 1989–90.

Christchurch Star

vessels. Russian, Korean and Taiwanese ships became a common sight in the inner harbour, and their crew members brought an international atmosphere to the port's pubs and bars. Another familiar sight in the inner harbour was the bright red vessels of the Pacifica Shipping Company, which had restarted a regular roll-on freight service between Lyttelton and Wellington in 1985.

While the city was stunned and saddened by the government's 1993 decision to close Wigram Airbase and move its pilot training to the North Island, leaving only a helicopter unit and the Airforce Museum as reminders that this was the birthplace of the RNZAF, Christchurch Airport has gone from strength to strength, coping with steadily increasing numbers of tourists. The advent of Ansett as a domestic competitor to Air New Zealand in 1987 brought a major addition to the domestic terminal, and the convenience of air bridges. The international end of the terminal was perennially overloaded, especially when two jumbo jets arrived together, and several extensions to the original building proved insufficient. In 1998 a new international arrivals building was opened where the Canterbury Aero Club's hangar once stood. New freight and postal facilities were added to the airport during this period, to handle increasing volumes of exports ranging from flowers and mushrooms to crayfish and venison.

Air pollution remained the city's number-one environmental problem in this period, and much public debate raged about its causes. Some people blamed diesel fumes from trucks and buses; others blamed the city's open domestic fires; yet others blamed the burning of damp wood in log-burner appliances.

Papanui Buildings in 1999, somehow diminished by a clutter of advertising and traffic signs. At least there are now trees to soften the urban landscape. (See pages 54, 78 and 91.)

But nobody could blame the thick coal smoke from steam trains or the gas-works any more. The city's air quality has been monitored since 1988, and no significant trends of increase or decrease in concentrations of winter pollutants have been found. Christchurch's love of log fires, coupled with rising electricity prices, seem likely to perpetuate its winter smog well into the new millennium.

Despite the smog, Christchurch people were living longer than ever before, and infant mortality declined in this period. Life expectancies for babies born in 1996 were 79 years for females and 73.5 for males, contrasting with figures a decade lower in the fifties, and an average age at death of less than 50 in 1919. Christchurch Hospital was rarely out of the news in these two decades, as health professionals questioned the wisdom of successive restructuring exercises in the health sector and resisted the move to commercial goals in hospital administration. As rural health services shrank and smaller hospitals closed, the city became increasingly important in the centralisation of regional health services. Christchurch Hospital was completely rebuilt in this period, with a succession of major buildings gradually replacing the old brick wards. The only survivors from the old hospital were the Nurses' Home (now converted into flats) and the Nurses' Memorial Chapel, which was saved only after a vigorous protest campaign.

The hills became highly desirably property for developers in this period, and not without controversy in some areas. Cashmere and Huntsbury suffered almost as much subdivision and infilling as Merivale or St Albans, where high land values made new residential units a profitable prospect, but a whole new hill suburb was developed further west at Westmorland even as new streets and luxury homes were added at the top of Cashmere Hill. Similar expansion and in-filling occurred at Mount Pleasant, St Andrews Hill and above Sumner, on Scarborough Hill. But most of the city's suburban expansion took place on the flat. Extensive new housing estates sprang up at Westlake, Broomfield, Hyde Park, Casebrook, Burwood and Parklands, as farmland was subdivided and former swamps were drained and filled to the north of the city. A new expressway, Queen Elizabeth II Drive, linked QEII Park and Travis Road to the Main North Road, giving easier access to the beaches of North New Brighton for residents of Redwood, Bishopdale and Papanui. As space filled up within the metropolitan area, those who preferred a rural setting (and could afford it) moved to 'lifestyle blocks' outside the city boundary.

In politics, Christchurch felt very much involved in central government in the eighties, having several of its MPs in the fourth Labour Cabinet, and then two prime ministers, however briefly, in 1990. But many Labour voters were also dismayed and disillusioned by Rogernomics and the wave of redundancies and unemployment that followed each round of state-sector restructuring. Historically a Labour stronghold, Sydenham became the home of the New Labour Party when Jim Anderton resigned from Labour in 1989 in protest at the government's apparent rejection of traditional Labour policies. National's return to power in 1990 prompted a combination of smaller parties in the Alliance Party in 1991, also led by Anderton until his resignation in 1994. He resumed its leadership in 1995, in time for New Zealand's first MMP election in 1996. The city's only Cabinet minister in the Bolger administration, Philip Burdon (Fendalton), retired at this election, which saw Gerry Brownlee elected to the new blue-ribbon seat of Ilam. Anderton won the new Wigram seat, and Mike

Mike Moore (1949–), Prime Minister of New Zealand, September–October 1990. MP for Eden 1972–75, Papanui 1978–84, Christchurch North 1984–96, Waimakariri 1996–99. Cabinet Minister 1984–90 and Leader of the Opposition 1990–93. Appointed Director-General of the World Trade Organisation in 1999.
Christchurch Star

Jim Anderton (1938–), MP for Sydenham since 1984. Leader of the Alliance Party. Labour Party President 1979–84. Formed New Labour Party, 1989. Former businessman and Auckland city councillor (twice mayoral candidate), he was named by *Time* magazine in 1974 as one of the world's 'outstanding young men'.
Christchurch Star

159

Sir Tipene O'Regan (1939–), chairman of Ngai Tahu Trust Board and chief negotiator for settlement of the tribe's Waitangi Tribunal claim. Chairman of the Maori Fisheries Commission and Sealord Fisheries, former director of TVNZ, prolific writer and lecturer: author of over a hundred reports to parliamentary select committees. Principal director of Aoraki Consultancy Services since 1983.

Christchurch Star

Moore took Waimakariri. Two Labour candidates, Tim Barnett and Larry Sutherland, held Christchurch Central and Christchurch East respectively, while the city gained seven new 'list' MPs. Thus the city remains largely left of centre in its political preferences, though its large middle-class vote is increasingly contested by National, ACT and New Zealand First.

Christchurch's economy is now broadly tripartite, comprising its traditional rural-based processing and export sector, an increasingly export-oriented manufacturing sector, and tourism. These combine to give the city a large commercial service sector, reflected in a strong growth of commercial floor space up to 1997. Businesses increased 44 per cent in Christchurch between 1991 and 1997, mostly in the financial and service sectors. The city now constitutes not only three-quarters of Canterbury's population, but contributes a large part of the South Island's economy. However, the city's economy is still sensitive to global trends, and the Asian financial crisis of 1997–98 caused the first serious fall in business confidence in a decade. Tourism remained buoyant, however. Unemployment was high in the early nineties, but had fallen along with the rest of New Zealand to about 6 per cent of the workforce by 1997. One worrying trend has been the steady increase in the long-term unemployed in Christchurch. Another is the higher rate of Maori unemployment in Christchurch. Maori adults comprise seven per cent of the Christchurch workforce, but thirteen per cent of the city's unemployed.

The success of the Ngai Tahu claim before the Waitangi Tribunal may change this situation for the better in the new millennium. The tribunal released its decision in 1991, finding that the Crown had been seriously in breach of its treaty obligations in failing to secure for Ngai Tahu the reserves it had been promised in the 1840s. In 1992 Ngai Tahu also won recognition of their extensive claim to fishing rights in South Island waters, and entered into a joint-venture purchase of Sealord Fisheries in lieu of a cash settlement. Finally, after many frustrating delays while the government tried to impose a billion-dollar cap on all Treaty claims, Ngai Tahu agreed in 1996 to accept $170 million, much of it in the form of Crown lands across the South Island. This settlement suddenly made Ngai Tahu a major player in the South Island's economy, and also in the economy of Christchurch. When Sir Tipene O'Regan signed the deed of settlement at Kaikoura in 1997, Ngai Tahu's investments had already made it a significant new force in Christchurch's property and business sectors, a role that looked likely to grow even larger in the new millennium.

As the city approaches the year 2000, Vicki Buck's successor as mayor, Garry Moore, has pledged to continue her proactive approach to the city's problems, and has the support of an experienced and hard-working set of councillors. As usual, major enhancement projects have proved controversial. The latest revamp of Cathedral Square has seen the replacement of New Zealand-produced terracotta tiles with expensive imported granite blocks, which dazzle the tourists in the Millennium Hotel. Although the City Council held a competition for the design of a new art gallery on the corner of Montreal Street and Worcester Boulevard, the winning (Australian) design, featuring a curved glass wall, has met with a mixed reception from citizens, and strong criticism from some local architects. On the other hand, one of the council's slogans won international recognition when Christchurch was voted 'Garden City of the World' in 1997.

The New Brighton Pier (second version) was completed in 1998, and the new public library beside the 1934 clock tower was opened on 24 July 1999.

Lancaster Park was renamed Jade Stadium in 1998 in recognition of its new corporate sponsor. The Hadlee Stand (1995) now overshadows the old Victory Park entrance (which is a war memorial), but is itself overshadowed by floodlight gantries (1995).

Nor'west arch, viewed from North Hagley Park. Heatherlea apartments at left.

What makes Christchurch different from other New Zealand cities? It certainly has a different 'feel' about it, partly from its physical setting, on a flat plain near the Port Hills, with the snow-capped Southern Alps in the distance. The pace of life is noticeably less frenetic than in Auckland or Wellington; the 'rush hour' is really just an hour, if that. But the main difference is probably in the people who live in and around Christchurch. Census returns show that Christchurch's population is slightly better educated than the rest of New Zealand, measured in terms of secondary, trade and tertiary qualifications. The proportion of the population without any school qualifications is lower than in New Zealand as a whole. The University of Canterbury claims to be the country's top research university, with internationally acclaimed experts in electronics and earthquake engineering, and many other scholars who are leaders in their fields. Lincoln Agricultural College became a university in its own right in 1990, and both institutions undertook major building programmes in the nineties, as did the Polytechnic, and attracted students from overseas as well as all

parts of New Zealand. With its well-educated workforce, Christchurch is poised to take advantage of the global revolution in information technology.

Perhaps the most important change in Christchurch since the seventies is that of attitude. Vicki Buck set the city a challenging example of leadership and problem-solving in her nine years as mayor. Nobody was ever in any doubt that she positively enjoyed making Christchurch a livelier and more interesting place than it had been when she was a schoolgirl. In business, in tourism, in the arts, there is a pervasive 'let's get on and *do* it' attitude about Christchurch in the late nineties, which has made it a much more interesting and successful city. And, despite the smog, it is still a very pleasant place for residents and tourists alike. It has many of the facilities and attractions of much larger cities, yet has the charm and convenience of an English cathedral town. The weather may be changeable, but it is usually predictable. And what other New Zealand city can offer the incomparable grandeur of that great curve of cloud and blue sky when the nor'wester blows?

FURTHER READING

Johannes C. Anderson, *Old Christchurch in Pictures and Story* (Christchurch: Simpson & Williams, 1949; reprinted by Capper Press, 1975)

John Cookson and Graeme Dunstall (eds), *Southern Capital* (Christchurch: Canterbury University Press, in press)

Stevan Eldred-Grigg, *A New History of Canterbury* (Dunedin: John McIndoe, 1982)

David Johnson, *Christchurch: A Pictorial History* (Christchurch: Canterbury University Press, 1992)

Joan Patricia Morrison, *The Evolution of a City: The Story of the Growth of the City and Suburbs of Christchurch, the Capital of Canterbury, in the Years from 1850 to 1903* (Christchurch: Christchurch City Council & Whitcombe and Tombs, 1948)

Robert C. Lamb, *From the Banks of the Avon: The Story of a River* (Wellington: Reed, 1981)

Gordon Ogilvie, *The Port Hills of Christchurch* (Wellington: Reed, 1978; reprinted by Philip King Booksellers, 1991)

Geoffrey W. Rice (ed.), *Christchurch Chronology: Significant Events in the History of Christchurch, New Zealand*, 3rd edition (Christchurch: Christchurch City Council, in press)

Philip Temple, *Christchurch, a City and its People* (Christchurch: Whitcombe and Tombs, 1973)

Henry Francis Wigram, *The Story of Christchurch, New Zealand* (Christchurch: Lyttelton Times Company, 1916)

John Wilson, *Christchurch: Swamp to City: A Short History of the Christchurch Drainage Board, 1875–1989* (Lincoln: Te Waihora Press, 1989)